Dublin

WHAT'S NEW | WHAT'S ON | WHAT'S BEST

www.timeout.com/dublin

Contents

Published by Time Out Guides Ltd
Universal House
251 Tottenham Court Road
London W1T 7AB
Tel: + 44 (0)20 7813 3000
Fax: + 44 (0)20 7813 6001
Email: guides@timeout.com
www.timeout.com

Managing Director Peter Fiennes
Editorial Director Ruth Jarvis
Business Manager Dan Allen
Editorial Manager Holly Pick
Assistant Management Accountant Ija Krasnikova

Time Out Guides is a wholly owned subsidiary of Time Out Group Ltd.

© Time Out Group Ltd
Chairman Tony Elliott
Group General Manager/Director Nichola Coulthard
Time Out Communications Ltd MD David Pepper
Time Out International Ltd MD Cathy Runciman
Time Out Magazine Ltd Publisher/MD Mark Elliott
Production Director Mark Lamond
Group IT Director Simon Chappell
Head of Marketing Catherine Demajo

Time Out and the Time Out logo are trademarks of Time Out Group Ltd.

This edition first published in Great Britain in 2008 by Ebury Publishing
A Random House Group Company
Company information can be found on www.randomhouse.co.uk
Random House UK Limited Reg. No. 954009
978-1-84670-095-8

Distributed in the US by Publishers Group West
Distributed in Canada by Publishers Group Canada

For further distribution details, see www.timeout.com

ISBN: 978-1-84670-104-7

A CIP catalogue record for this book is available from the British Library.

Printed and bound in Germany by Appl.

The Random House Group Limited supports The Forest Stewardship Council (FSC), the
leading international forest certification organisation. All our titles that are printed on
Greenpeace approved FSC certified paper carry the FSC logo. Our paper procurement
policy can be found at www.rbooks.co.uk/environment.

Time Out carbon-offsets all its flights with Trees for Cities (www.treesforcities.org).

Dublin Shortlist

The **Time Out Dublin Shortlist 2009** is one of a new series of guides that draws on Time Out's background as a magazine publisher to keep you current with everything that's going on in town. As well as Dublin's key sights and the best of its eating, drinking and leisure options, it picks out the most exciting venues to have opened recently and gives a full calendar of events. It also includes features on the important news, trends and openings, all compiled by locally based editors and writers. Whether you're visiting for the first time in your life or the first time this year, you'll find the *Time Out Dublin Shortlist* contains all you need to know, in a portable and easy-to-use format.

The guide divides central Dublin into seven areas, each containing listings for Sights & Museums, Eating & Drinking, Shopping, Nightlife and Arts & Leisure, and maps pinpointing their locations. At the front of the book are chapters rounding up these scenes city-wide, and giving a shortlist of our overall picks. We also include itineraries for days out, plus essentials such as transport information and hotels.

Our listings give phone numbers as dialled within Dublin. From abroad, use your country's exit code followed by 353 (the country code for Ireland) plus 1 (the area code for Dublin) and then the number given.

We have noted price categories by using one to four euro signs (€-€€€€), representing budget, moderate, expensive and luxury. Major credit cards are accepted unless otherwise stated. We also indicate when a venue is NEW.

All our listings are double-checked, but places do sometimes close or change their hours or prices, so it's a good idea to call a venue before visiting. While every effort has been made to ensure accuracy, the publishers cannot accept responsibility for any errors that this guide may contain.

Venues are marked on the maps using symbols numbered according to their order within the chapter and colour-coded as follows:

❶ Sights & Museums
❶ Eating & Drinking
❶ Shopping
❶ Nightlife
❶ Arts & Leisure

Map key

Major sight or landmark	▪
Railway station	▪
Park	▪
Hospital	▪
Neighbourhood	RANELAGH
Pedestrian street	▭
Main road	—
Church	✚
Airport	✈
Luas	Ⓛ
Luas under construction	Ⓛ

Time Out Dublin Shortlist

EDITORIAL
Editor Simon Cropper
Deputy Editor Claire Boobbyer
Proofreader Jo Willacy

DESIGN
Art Director Scott Moore
Art Editor Pinelope Kourmouzoglou
Senior Designer Henry Elphick
Graphic Designers Kei Ishimaru,
Nicola Wilson
Advertising Designer Jodi Sher
Picture Editor Jael Marschner
Deputy Picture Editor Lynn Chambers
Picture Researcher Gemma Walters
Picture Desk Assistant Marzena Zoladz
Picture Librarian Christina Theisen

ADVERTISING
Commercial Director Mark Phillips
Sales Manager (GB & Ireland)
Alison Wallen
Advertising Sales Hot Sales Ltd, Dublin

MARKETING
Marketing Manager Yvonne Poon
**Sales & Marketing Director, North
America & Latin America** Lisa Levinson
Senior Publishing Brand Manager
Luthfa Begum
Marketing Designers Anthony Huggins

PRODUCTION
Production Manager Brendan McKeown
Production Controller Damian Bennett
Production Co-ordinator Julie Pallot

CONTRIBUTORS
This guide was researched and written by Ron Pasas, Marianne Power, Daragh Reddin
and the writers of Time Out Dublin. The editor would like to thank Fiona Dowling, Ger
Kenny and Sam Le Quesne.

PHOTOGRAPHY
Photography by Alys Tomlinson; except pages 8, 9, 38, 39, 41, 54, 66, 69, 83, 86,
87, 95, 144, 145 Britta Jaschinski; page 31 Sportsfile; page 35 Colm Mullen; page 48
© Mr Brendan Dempsey, Audio Visual and Media Services, Trinity College Dublin; page
80 ESB/Number 29; page 99 (top) Anthony Woods; page 99 (bottom) Tom Lawler;
page 107 NMS Photography Ltd; page 112 Mark McCall 2008; page 121 courtesy Irish
Museum of Modern Art.

The following pictures were supplied by the featured establishments/artists: pages 36,
53, 120, 127.

Cover photograph: © Jean-Pierre Lescourret/SuperStock

MAPS
JS Graphics (john@jsgraphics.co.uk).

About Time Out

Founded in 1968, Time Out has expanded from humble London beginnings into the
leading resource for those wanting to know what's happening in the world's greatest
cities. As well as our influential what's-on weeklies in London, New York and Chicago,
we publish more than a dozen other listings magazines in cities as varied as Beijing
and Mumbai. The magazines established Time Out's trademark style: sharp writing,
informed reviewing and bang up-to-date inside knowledge of every scene.

Time Out made the natural leap into travel guides in the 1980s with the City Guide
series, which now extends to over 50 destinations around the world. Written and
researched by expert local writers and generously illustrated with original photography,
the full-size guides cover a larger area than our Shortlist guides and include many more
venue reviews, along with additional background features and a full set of maps.

Throughout this rapid growth, the company has remained proudly independent, still
owned by Tony Elliott four decades after he started Time Out London as a single fold-out
sheet of A5 paper. This independence extends to the editorial content of all
our publications, this Shortlist included. No establishment has been featured because
it has advertised, and no payment has influenced any of our reviews. And, for our critics,
there's definitely no such thing as a free lunch: all restaurants and bars are visited
and reviewed anonymously, and Time Out always picks up the bill.
For more about the company, see www.timeout.com.

Don't Miss

Marsh's Library p11

WHAT'S BEST
Sights & Museums

People come to Dublin for the sea, the scenery, the culture, and the *craic* – that untranslatable Gaelic oxymoron, which means something like 'frenzied, laid-back fun'. It's all present and correct, of course: the tour buses still do the rounds, the pubs still serve perfect pints of Guinness, and the place still works its reliable magic. But should you be returning to the city after an interval of several years, you're likely to notice some changes.

The conversation in the bars and newspapers may revolve around the themes of recession and the tightening of belts, but the Dublin you see today still bears the marks of the recent boom. It has become conspicuously multicultural: home to large groups of Polish, Lithuanian, Nigerian and Chinese; you can buy olive oil in corner shops, sushi in supermarkets and exotic spices in specialist shops; and you can drink beer, whiskey, alcopops or whatever you fancy in nightclubs until 2.30am.

What's more, as if in defiance of the global financial crisis, the city has gained a generous splattering of new buildings and bridges and swanky renovations, either just opened or about to open: Dublin City Council's office building next to City Hall (p58) was completed in mid 2008; the chq (p114), a former industrial tobacco warehouse underwent a €40 million redevelopment in 2007 and now houses shops and restaurants; and the Docklands area is a buzzing

SHORTLIST

Best new
- Science Gallery (p51)

Best overview
- Dublinia (p59)

Best arty
- Chester Beatty Library (p55)
- Irish Museum of Modern Art (p116)
- National Gallery of Ireland (p77)
- National Museum of Ireland: Decorative Arts & History (p103)

Best holy
- Christ Church Cathedral (p58)
- St Michan's Church (p104)
- St Patrick's Cathedral (p59)

Best bookish
- Old Library & Book of Kells (p50)

Best historic
- Dublin Castle (p59)
- Jeanie Johnston (p114)
- Kilkenny Castle (p129)
- Kilmainham Gaol (p117)
- Liberty Hall (p111)
- National Museum of Archaeology & History (p77)

Best prehistoric
- Newgrange (p129)

Best for the young
- Dublin Zoo (p102)
- Imaginosity (p127)
- Science Gallery (p51)

Best views
- Dalkey (p123)
- St Canice's Cathedral (p129)
- Wicklow Mountains (p132)

Best booze
- Guinness Storehouse (p116)
- Old Jameson Distillery (p104)

Best open air
- Phoenix Park (p104)
- Sandymount (p127)

Best secret
- Ardgillen Castle (p125)

hive of new projects, from arts venues to hotels and bridges – including Santiago Calatrava's Samuel Beckett Bridge, which looks like a harp.

In other words, Dublin is a city with the power to confirm expectations and defy them at the same time; and as recession bites, it will have to find more inventive (and more affordable) reasons for people to visit. This is a great time to come to Dublin.

The right approach

When you think of its large reputation, Dublin's physical dimensions are surprisingly modest. The city centre comprises just a few manageably sized neighbourhoods, bisected by the Liffey, and you'll find that it's no distance at all from the top of O'Connell Street (on the north side of the river) to the peaceful Grand Canal on the south side.

Ancient. Treasures. Modern. Pleasures.

Surprising. Exciting. Revealing. Inviting.

Priceless. Precious. Timeless and free.

In a word - Extraordinary

museum

National Museum of Ireland
Ard-Mhúsaem na hÉireann

Archaeology
Natural History   (Closed until further notice, see www.museum.ie)
Decorative Arts & History
Country Life

Free Admission. Tuesday to Saturday 10am to 5pm, Sunday 2pm to 5pm. Closed Mondays. Tel (01) 6777 444. Family Programmes & Events for People of All Ages. Visit www.museum.ie

National Gallery p77

By far the best way to set about exploring the place is on foot. If you've brought a car, park it right now and try never to think of it again unless you're heading out of town – the traffic is too heavy and the town too small to make driving enjoyable. All you need are the maps we've supplied in the main listings chapters, a bit of sunshine (not all that rare in these parts, despite the jokes) and a pair of comfortable shoes.

Past, present, future

Despite its compact layout, Dublin packs in a good deal of variety. There are historic buildings by the dozen, many famous, others, like the impressive Marsh's Library (St Patrick's Close, 454 3511, www. marshlibrary.ie), less so; plenty of green spaces and quiet squares; and enough shops, bars and restaurants to gobble up your holiday allowance ten times over.

In other words, it's a city with a strong sense of its past (it seems that every few steps bring you to another statue, another heritage plaque announcing the birth place of this playwright or the first home of that poet).

And yet, an equal portion of its landscape has been set in the future, with a crop of modern structures and buildings contending with the Georgian terraces and the ancient bell towers – of these, O'Connell Street's Spire is undoubtedly the most recognisable, whereas the many signature bridges that span the Liffey and the multimillion euro developments and regeneration projects from Smithfield to Docklands are waiting to be discovered.

The lie of the land

Most of the action is concentrated in and around the two most central neighbourhoods, Temple Bar

(pp55-72) and St Stephen's Green (pp73-88). The former, a maze of tiny cobbled streets and busy thoroughfares, is home to a tight scrum of bars, restaurants, night spots and trendy shops. It's also home to the city's two major cathedrals, St Patrick's (p59) and Christ Church (p58) – but somehow, it copes admirably with its personality clash of holiness and consumerism, and although the juxtaposition of awe-inspiring monuments to Christianity and raucous parties of staggering stags has caused friction among the locals, it seems to go pretty much without a hitch as far as visitors are concerned. The rule of thumb is simple: if you want to raise hell, hit the pubs and clubs of Temple Bar after dark; if it's heaven you're interested in, stick to the cathedrals.

More sophisticated by far is the neighbouring St Stephen's Green with its clutch of excellent museums around Kildare Street, notably the National Museum of Archaeology & History (p77) and the treasure trove of fine art that is the National Gallery of Ireland (p77). And for consumer culture, this is Dublin's epicentre, thanks

to nearby Grafton Street with its shops, cafés and restaurants.

The other main shopping hub is O'Connell Street (and its tributary, the ever-busy Henry Street), which culminates in a spearhead of excellent museums dotted around Parnell Square, most notably the Hugh Lane Gallery (p90). To the west of here is the up-and-coming Smithfield (p102) and, further still, the vast Phoenix Park (p104), also home to Dublin Zoo (p102). Just across the bridge to the south is the formidable campus of Trinity College (p48), with its ancient claim to fame in pride of place in the Old Library & Book of Kells (p50). And finally, to the east is the heady mix of past, present and future that is the city's Docklands (p110).

Making the most of it

The Dublin Pass (www.dublinpass. ie), is a smart card which, for a fee, gets you in free to sights across the city. How affordable it is depends on how much you plan to see – prices start at €31 for a one-day card to €89 for a six-day pass.

For information on Dublin's public transport, see p148. For tourist information, see p156.

St Stephen's Green

Cake Café p79

WHAT'S BEST
Eating & Drinking

When it comes to dining out, Dublin isn't London, Paris or New York. Nevertheless, it has a much better range of good food, local and international, than it had ten years ago; standards of service and presentation have also improved considerably; and in these straitened times, many menus are very reasonably priced. You can make a tasty, nourishing meal in a growing number of cafés, or splash a bucketful of cash on dinner in one of the city's world-class haute cuisine addresses. These days, you can also sit down to growing multicultural cuisine. And when it's time for a drink, the pubs and bars are not just world-class, they're world-beaters.

Dining out

After years of exuberant and extravagant new dining concepts, finally, it seems, the city's restaurateurs have realised that style over substance is a recipe for short-term success only, and that good food needs integrity, not just an advertising budget. As ever, the fine-dining sector is working hard – Dublin has some truly stellar restaurants for people who have the time and funds, places like Restaurant Patrick Guilbaud (p84) and Thornton's (p67) – but the good news is that casual neighbourhood restaurants are also attracting praise from critics and consumers – establishments such as Bang Café (p78), Town

Bar and Grill (p67) and Cornucopia (p62). Another notable trend is the rise of the affordable overseas options, especially around the Quartier Bloom – places like Enoteca delle Langhe (p93) and Charming Noodle (p95).

And when it comes to the waiters, word spreads quickly if a restaurant is not up to scratch. Snooty service, especially prevalent during the boom years, has been replaced with better training and management. Customers have been clamouring for better value, more fun and dishes they can enjoy – and now they're getting it all.

Café society

Dubliners still remember the time when the average cup of coffee served in a café here would be the colour and approximate flavour of tepid dishwater. But as Dublin grew more prosperous, standards rose: new cafés began to sprout on every corner, and tepid dishwater was no longer enough.

Yes, Dubliners have embraced caffeine culture like a long-lost friend. Whether it's their unique atmosphere, superior coffee or simply the fact that the staff are happy to let you linger for hours reading or chatting, Dublin's cafés provide a welcome alternative to the major chains: two establishments not to be missed are the historic Bewley's Oriental Café (p61) and the newcomer everyone's talking about, Bald Barista (p59).

Raising a glass (or two)

It's hard to think of another city in the world as synonymous with its pubs and bars as Dublin. The St James's Gate brewery (despite its imminent downsizing) is famous the world over, and visiting divas

DON'T MISS

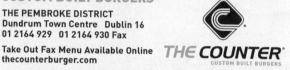

and dignitaries, even if they know nothing else about Ireland, can always be relied on to pose for the press with a glass of Guinness in their hands.

Dublin author Brendan Behan called himself 'a drinker with a writing problem'; Oscar Wilde averred that 'work is the curse of the drinking classes'; and actor Richard Harris claimed to have formed Alcoholics Unanimous. 'If you don't feel like a drink, you ring another member and he comes over to persuade you.' For sure, this is the city that launched a thousand quips. So it should come as no surprise then to learn that Dublin has no shortage of bars, superpubs, dingy boozers and dives in which to pass the time of day, or just to wait for the next break in the rain.

What's more, recession is grist for the mill for Irish barflies; and, as you'll quickly discover, economic hardship provides the subject matter for 90 per cent of Irish drinking songs.

If what you're looking for is a pub with a bit of craic, you almost cannot go wrong. The streets surrounding Grafton Street and Dawson Street are where Dublin's more fashion-conscious drinkers like to rest their Prada bags and sip Cosmopolitans. South from George's Street to Wexford Street and on to Camden Street there are dozens of bars popular with a younger, hipper crowd. Temple Bar at night is almost strictly the preserve of British hen and stag parties, and the joints around Trinity College attract middle-aged tourists by the busload.

But there are exceptions to each of these rules, so we suggest you pick a bar from our Shortlist that sounds like your kind of place, regardless of where it happens to be located.

Winding Stair p98

Brown Thomas p68

WHAT'S BEST
Shopping

The retail industry is positively thriving in Dublin, economic downturn or not, and the excellent choice of shops runs from smart, cosmopolitan delis to quirky record stores. The city holds its own against other European capitals when it comes to the presence of big chain stores and heavyweight designers, but Dublin still retains an independent edge: check out its seductive little boutiques and Irish labels to see what we mean.

Part of Dublin's appeal is its handy size. It's compact and navigable, so walking from one shopping area to another is a pleasure; and if you weary of the urban scene, you can jump on a Luas and rub shoulders with the suburbanites at the mammoth Dundrum Town Centre (Sandyford Road, Dundrum, 299 1700, www.dundrum.ie).

In the city, a good place to start south of the River Liffey is Grafton Street. A smart pedestrianised thoroughfare, it draws eager consumers and hopeful buskers in equal measure, and is lined with a good selection of chain stores and shoe shops. Avoid it mid afternoon at the weekend, though, unless you enjoy fighting through huge crowds. For a taste of upmarket Dublin, try the very elegant Brown Thomas (p68), a super-chic department store devoted to the world's most exclusive labels.

Nearby William Street South, Castle Market and Drury Street offer a hipper, trendier slice of retail life, with independent boutiques and a slower pace, and the pleasant jumble of George's Street Arcade is ideal for unearthing unusual second-hand gear, from books to bell-bottoms. Head down to the Old City at the northern edge of Temple Bar, and you'll find the compendious Urban Outfitters (4 Cecilia Street), top food shop Fallon & Byrne (p68), a clutch of hip little stores, and, on Saturdays from 10am to 5pm, the fashionable Cow Lane Market. If it's antiques you're after, Francis Street, in the Liberties district, is a deceptively low-key road that sells some of Ireland's best paintings and antique furniture.

North of the river lies the busy and shop-filled Henry Street, the Jervis Centre (p98) and the newly spruced-up ILAC (p97), a formerly run-down shopping centre that has been renovated. Vastly less pretentious than the southside, the northside has a different atmosphere, and Moore Street, with its old-school market traders, offers a glimpse into the Dublin of old.

Feeling fashionable

The area around Grafton Street has some of the city's best boutiques – places like Tulle (28 Georges Street Arcade, 679 9115), Smock (p68), and Dolls (32 Clarendon Street, 672 9004), all treasure troves of designer dresses and achingly hip accessories – and all very expensive. For more affordable togs, try Sabotage (Exchequer Street, 670 4789), popular with twentysomethings looking for a designery dress at a high street price. If it's Irish designers you're looking for, Louise Kennedy has her own shop (p86), and also sells through Brown Thomas. For men, Louis Copeland (p109) is Ireland's best known tailor.

Traditional taste

Since its recent revamp, Blarney
Woollen Mills (p52) has lost its
tourist vibe, and is now a great
source of quality, modern
knitwear. Avoca (p67) is the Irish
Cath Kidston, where old-world
food, fashion and homewares
become cool; it stocks a lovely
collection of bright mohair rugs,
gorgeous ornaments and lovely
jams. And if it's a piece of crystal
you're after, Kilkenny (Nassau
Street, 677 7066) has the best
selection: its range includes
pieces by Paul Costelloe and
Louise Kennedy. Kilkenny also
has a good collection of young
Irish clothes designers, including
handbag queen Orla Kiely, as well
as Newbridge silver and great Irish
pottery by Stephen Pearce.

Books

Ireland is a nation of scholars and
poets, as you're immediately aware
whenever you walk into a
bookshop. Hodges Figgis (p68) is
considered the best in Dublin, and
was even mentioned in *Ulysses*, but
the smaller establishments are just
as worthy. Books Upstairs (p67)
is an independent store loved by
writers and academics tuned into all
things Irish; the massive Chapters
(Ivy Exchange, Parnell Street, 872
3297) also has a fine second-hand
section and has recently been given
a serious makeover. Finally, the
rickety Winding Stair (p98) simply
drips with charm, and has for years
been an informal drop-in centre for
intellectuals who used to take books
from the shelves to the coffee shop
upstairs (now a lovely restaurant).

Opening hours and tax refunds

Shops are generally open from
9am to 6pm Monday to Saturday,
and from around noon to 6pm on
Sunday. Almost all stores stay
open late on Thursday – usually
until 8pm or 9pm.

MasterCard and Visa credit
cards are widely accepted;
AmEx and Diners Club cards
are generally only accepted in
the bigger stores.

Sales tax (VAT) is 21 per cent;
visitors from outside the EU can
get a refund at the airport.

Fallon & Byrne p68

The George p71

Nightlife

A decade ago, Dublin established itself as one of Europe's top party destinations. By the time Britney, J-Lo et al rolled into town for the MTV Music Awards in 1999, the city could claim to be the going out capital of Europe. That was before its crown was snatched by quirkier, cheaper cities like Tallinn and Prague.

Then, in August 2008, despite loud protests, Facebook petitions and a campaign called Give Us the Night, the Irish government closed the loophole that had allowed some clubs with theatre licences to stay open well after 3am. Never despair: a typical weekend in Dublin will show that when it comes to letting their hair down, the Irish are still up there with the best.

Rock, jazz & Irish

Not so long ago, the way locals felt about the city's music scene was summed up by the ubiquitous graffito 'Dublin is Dead'. Happily, things are now looking up. The last few years have seen a burst of live music in the capital, and the hunger for new acts and new tunes is being fed with a steady stream of exciting local and imported bands.

Most rock and jazz venues are conveniently located in or around the city centre. A few of them, such as the Helix (www.thehelix.ie) and the National Stadium, are deep in the suburbs – but even those are only 30 minutes from the centre by bus. Large rock concerts are occasionally held in outdoor venues like Punchestown

S H O R T L I S T

Best new
- Andrews Lane (p68)
- Crawdaddy (p87)
- O2 (p114)
- Think Tank (p71)
- Tripod (p87)

Best bands
- Ballroom of Romance (p86)
- Pravda (p100)
- Vicar Street (p108)
- Whelan's (p88)

Best DJs
- Academy (p99)
- Kennedy's (p52)
- Solas (p87)

Best gay
- George (p71)
- Pantibar (p108)
- Purty Kitchen (p71)

Best sound systems
- Button Factory (p71)
- Olympia (p71)
- Vicar Street (p109)

The all-rounders
- Gaiety (p71)
- Sugar Club (p87)

The early bird
- Solas (p87)

Lovin' it large
- Ambassador (p99)
- O2 (p114)

Jaaaaazz
- Hugh Lane (p99)
- JJ Smyth's (p71)
- Vicar Street (p109)

Global sounds
- Liberty Hall Theatre (p111)

For old time glamour
- Olympia (p71)

Best booze
- JJ Smyth's (p71)
- Pravda (p100)
- Purty Kitchen (p71)

racecourse, Croke Park (now the default venue while Lansdowne Road is being done up) and the RDS (www.rds.ie).

Inside the city boundary, venues like the International Bar (p64) have done much to boost the profile of such quality acts as Gemma Hayes, Adrian Crowley and Paddy Casey; and then there's the crop of brand new venues, the Village (p85), Liberty Hall (p111), Crawdaddy (p87) and Andrews Lane (p68), all supplying a local audience with hot new sounds. At the upper end of the scale, the former Point Theatre reopened in December 2008 as O2 (p114), expanded and greatly improved after an 18-month refurb.

Still, the old venues can be just as good as new, and most music fans feel that Whelan's (p88), one of the most prestigious venues in the city, remains the best place at which to catch Dublin's brightest rising stars.

The best guides to enjoying London life

(but don't just take our word for it)

'Armed with a tube map and this guide there is no excuse to find yourself in a duff bar again'

Evening Standard

'I'm always asked how I keep up to date with shopping and services in a city as big as London. This guide is the answer'

Red Magazine

'You will never again be stuck for interesting things to do and places to visit in the capital'

Independent on Sunday

Rated 'Best Restaurant Guide'

Sunday Times

TIME OUT GUIDES WRITTEN BY LOCAL EXPERTS
timeout.com/shop

When it comes to traditional Irish music, Dublin can still knock out some of the best and most exciting performers in the country. The last decade has seen the rise of a new generation of such acts (Lunasa, Solas, Martin Hayes and Dennis Cahill, Karen Casey and North Cregg); and then there are bands like Kila, which combines Irish trad with influences from Africa, the Far East and South America. If you fancy a taste of Irish while you're here, head over to Claddagh Records (p68), which helps convert local success stories to national and international acclaim – and also sells tickets.

Nightclubs

Dublin's clubbers are a discerning bunch, and the nightclub scene includes a dynamic variety of venues – but you need to know where to look to find the best. Luckily, most of the top clubs are within ten minutes' walk from the banks of the Liffey. On the south side, the best cluster is around South Great George's Street and Wicklow Street – places like gay club George (p71) and, in particular, the hot newcomer Andrews Lane (p68), housed in what used to be a theatre. On the north side, the pattern is a little more scattered, but Abbey Street, just off O'Connell Street, has some interesting addresses – check out Academy (p99) or the Russia-themed Pravda (p100).

One area to steer well clear of is Temple Bar. Once the centre of the clubbing universe, it's now largely dead; locals only recommend it to the sort of tourists they don't want to see in their favourite clubs.

The lowdown

For full listings of concerts in Dublin, pick up the free *Event Guide* in bars, cafés and record shops – or check out Irish music promoter Comhaltas's website, http://comhaltas.ie.

When it comes to buying tickets, places like the O2, Whelan's and Olympia (p71) have their own box offices, but other major venues and smaller but established names like Vicar Street (p108) rely on agencies. Ticketmaster (0818 719 300/from outside Ireland 456 9569/ www.ticketmaster.ie), in the St Stephen's Green shopping centre, deals with just about every big event; the Tourism Centre on Suffolk Street can make credit card bookings (605 7729/www.visit dublin.com); and tickets can often be bought at record shops. If in doubt, phone the venue to learn the best source of tickets.

Tripod p87

Project
Arts Centre p72

WHAT'S BEST
Arts & Leisure

Dubliners are cultured people, and the arts scene – already pretty strong – is improving in leaps and bounds pretty much across the board. The venues are getting better, more numerous and more adventurous; and the range of artists who put on shows of one kind or another is increasingly international.

Visual arts

The local market for Irish art is as buoyant as ever, and galleries new and old seem to be raking in the cash. Dublin's commercial galleries are clustered in two areas: Temple Bar, which also has one of the city's most innovative non-commercial spaces, the Project Arts Centre (p72); and Grafton Street and St Stephen's Green, where you'll find the Rubicon (p88) for contemporary art, and the excellent Gorry (p72) for more traditional work.

The city also has a thriving set of underground exhibition spaces – many housed in inconspicuous Georgian buildings, converted stables and renovated warehouses; these alternative art dens often let the viewer engage with the work in the same place where they were created. One notable newcomer on this scene is the maverick Monster Truck (p120), which favours a 'machine gun' approach whereby new work is displayed at least three times a month.

But perhaps the best example of the DIY culture that's catching on in Dublin is the purchase of the Bernard Shaw (11 South Richmond

Street, 712 8342, www.bodytonic
music.com) by local promoters
Bodytonic. As well as a series of
exhibitions, this 114-year-old pub
hosts regular screenings, record
fairs, computer game competitions
and experimental music – not to
mention occasional unannounced
appearances by high-profile DJs.

Theatre

Dublin's theatrical landscape is
shifting. In 2008, the much-loved
Andrews Lane Theatre closed its
doors to become, of all things, a
nightclub (p68), and the grand
old Abbey (p100) is pushing ahead
with plans to move to plush new
quarters in Docklands, where it will
get an illustrious neighbour in the
form of Daniel Libeskind's Grand
Canal Theatre. And in more modest
ventures, the Gaiety (p71) and the
Gate (p101) have recently spent
millions of euros on spiffy refurbs.

Classics from the Irish canon –
*The Importance of Being Earnest,
Waiting for Godot* and the like – are
performed with steady regularity
and varying quality by the Abbey
and the Gate. The best bets for new,
avant-garde work are the Peacock
in the Abbey (p100) and the Project
Arts Centre, which host independent
experimental companies such as
Dance Theatre of Ireland.

Dance

There's Riverdance and there's
dance. Dance companies in Ireland
continue to struggle, because
although the Irish are undoubtedly
partial to watching their children
hop around in traditional outfits,
there's no tradition of sitting still
on seats and watching dancers on
stage. (Traditional Irish dancing is
still a big thing, but not in Dublin
– although you can still stumble
across the odd impromptu session.)

SHORTLIST

Best new
- Gallery Number One (p72)
- Royal Hibernian Gallery (p88)

Irish drama
- Abbey (p100)
- Gaiety (p71)

Contemporary drama
- Gate (p101)

Contemporary art
- Cross Gallery (p120)
- Green on Red (p54)
- Hillsboro Gallery (p101)
- Monster Truck (p120)
- Taylor Galleries (p88)

Older art
- Gorry Gallery (p72)
- Taylor Galleries (p88)

Artists' studios
- Royal Hibernian Gallery (p88)
- Temple Bar Gallery (p72)

Best snaps
- Gallery of Photography (p72)

Best footwork
- Irish Modern Dance
  Theatre (p72)

Best motion pictures
- Cineworld (p100)
- Irish Film Institute (p72)
- Light House (p109)
- Savoy (p101)

Best classical music
- Gaiety (p71)
- National Concert Hall (p88)

Most multidisciplined
- O2 (p114)
- Project Arts Centre (p72)
- Tivoli (p120)

Best festivals
- Dublin Dance Festival (p31)
- Dublin Theatre Festival (p34)
- Dublin Writers Festival (p31)
- Jameson Dublin International
  Film Festival (p34)

DON'T MISS

A short-lived Irish national ballet company dissolved in 1989 and there hasn't been one since; in its stead, a few small, dedicated and talented companies – like the aforementioned Dance Theatre of Ireland (www.dancetheatreireland.com) – keep the art alive.

Classical music & opera

Though Dublin music buffs are fond of the fact that Handel's *Messiah* had its premiere here in 1742, the city's contribution to classical music is largely undistinguished. The city has no opera house, and despite the occasional success of productions such as *Salomé* and *Tosca* at the Gaiety, Dublin doesn't compare with other European cities.

Still, the situation is far from hopeless. Though classical music doesn't have the high profile of other art forms here, there's still plenty being performed. The National Concert Hall (p88) is home to the RTÉ Concert Orchestra and the National Symphony Orchestra; and performances by contemporary chamber ensembles such as Vox 21, the Crash Ensemble and popular choir Anúna can often be seen at the likes of the Project Arts Centre.

Information & tickets

The *Dublin Event Guide* and Thursday's *Irish Times* contain listings and reviews; the *Dubliner* carries reviews of the bigger productions. Most Dublin theatres and companies produce their own leaflets, which can usually be found in tourist centres, hotels and cafés. In addition, the *Golden Pages* phone directory has a particularly useful theatre information section.

Film

The Irish Film Institute (p72) is an excellent starting point for an exploration of Ireland's film heritage; the Light House (p109) is where you can catch the maverick and offbeat. The other city-centre cinemas are multiplexes offering the usual fare.

The city hosts a number of annual festivals, including the Dublin International Lesbian & Gay Film Festival (www.gaze.ie), and the Dark/Light Festival (www.darklight-filmfestival.com) in May or June, which focuses on digital movies by up-and-coming film-makers. A recent addition is the Jameson International Dublin Film Festival, which offers a great mix of Irish, international, mainstream and offbeat fare.

PEACOCK

THE BROTHERS SIZE

Abbey p100

Calendar

Dublin City Marathon p36

This is the pick of events that had been announced as we went to press. You'd do well to book your hotel at least a couple of months in advance if you plan to visit when one of the bigger festivals or sporting events is taking place – it can be almost impossible to find accommodation when the Six Nations rugby tournament is playing, for example.

January

Late Jan **Temple Bar TradFest**
Various venues
templebartrad.com
A feast of traditional Irish music and culture. See box p35.

February

Mid Feb **Six Nations Rugby**
Croke Park
www.irishrugby.ie

This rugby tournament is one of the biggest events in the Irish calendar. The mood on match days is electric.

Mid Feb **Jameson Dublin International Film Festival**
Various venues
www.dubliniff.com
Celebrates the best of Irish and world cinema across the city, with chances to meet writers, directors and actors.

March

Mar **12 Points! Festival of Europe's New Jazz**
Various venues
www.project.ie/www.improvised music.ie/12points.php
A sassy mix of jazz from all points of the European compass; movies, workshops and exhibitions too.

17 Mar **St Patrick's Day Parade & Festival**
Across the city
www.stpatricksfestival.ie

Time Out
Travel Guides

British Isles

**Written by
local experts**

Mid June **Future Days**
Various venues
www.foggynotions.ie
Hip new rock bands. See box p35.

Mid June **Pride**
Various venues
www.dublinpride.org
A week-long gay festival: céilidh, drag contests, and the Pride march itself.

16 June **Bloomsday Festival**
James Joyce Centre
www.jamesjoyce.ie
A week of Joycean readings, performances, excursions and more.

June-Aug **Music in the Park**
Various venues
www.dublincity.ie
Laid-back jazz or rousing opera in the city's parks – and it's all free.

July 2009

Ongoing Music in the Park

10-12 July **Oxegen**
Punchestown Racecourse
www.oxegen.ie/www.mcd.ie
Multi-stage rock festival. See box p35.

Mid July **Analog**
Docklands
www.analogconcerts.ie
Top music, top writers. See box p35.

Mid July **Dublin Circus Festival**
Various venues
www.templebar.ie
Roll up for a mix of performance art and traditional circus skills.

August 2009

5-9 Aug **Dublin Horse Show**
Royal Dublin Society
www.dublinhorseshow.com
Five-day showjumping event that pulls in high-profile visitors and competitors; includes the famous Nations' Cup.

28-30 Aug **Festival of World Cultures**
Various venues
www.festivalofworldcultures.com
Arts and music festival in which over 50 countries take part. See box p35.

Maritime Festival p31

September 2009

Early-late Sept **Dublin Fringe Festival**
Various venues
www.fringefest.com
Performances, often from new companies, and in all kinds of venues.

4-6 Sept **Electric Picnic**
Stradbally Estate
www.electricpicnic.ie
Modern music galore. See box p35.

12, 26 Sept **All-Ireland Hurling & Football Finals**
Croke Park
www.gaa.ie
The hurling and Gaelic football finals.

Mid September **Hard Working Class Heroes**
Various venues
www.hwch.net
Hip new rock bands. See box p35.

Mid September **Liffey Swim**
Rory O'More Bridge to Custom
House Quay
www.dublincity.ie
Famous annual river swimming race
that draws 400 foolhardy entrants.

24 Sept-11 Oct **Dublin Theatre
Festival**
Various venues
www.dublintheatrefestival.com
The best of Irish and world theatre.
Be sure to book well ahead.

October 2009

Ongoing Dublin Theatre Festival

22-25 Oct **Dublin Electronic
Arts Festival**
deafireland.com
Where sparks fly. See box p35.

26 Oct **Adidas Dublin City
Marathon**
www.dublincitymarathon.ie
The 26-mile (42km) course starts and
finishes at the top of O'Connell Street.

31 Oct **Samhain Festival
(Hallowe'en)**
Various venues
www.visitdublin.com
The pagan festival of Samhain ('sow
in') is a celebration of the dead marked
by a parade and great fireworks.

December 2009

24 Dec **Christmas Eve Vigil**
St Mary's Pro-Cathedral
A vigil is held by the Archbishop of
Dublin, with the beautiful sounds of
the Palestrina Choir.

25, 26 Dec **Christmas Day
& St Stephen's Day**
On Christmas Day, shops, restaurants,
pubs and public transport close down.
On St Stephen's Day, pubs reopen and
the day ends with a big party.

January 2010

Late Jan **Temple Bar TradFest**
Various venues
templebartrad.com
A feast of traditional Irish music and
culture. See box p35.

February 2010

Feb **Six Nations Rugby**
Croke Park
www.irishrugby.ie
This rugby tournament is one of the
biggest events in the Irish calendar.
The mood on match days is electric.

Mid Feb **Jameson Dublin
International Film Festival**
Various venues
www.dubliniff.com
Celebrates the best of Irish and world
cinema across the city, with chances to
meet writers, directors and actors.

March 2010

Mar **12 Points! Festival of
Europe's New Jazz**
Various venues
*www.project.ie/www.improvised
music.ie/12points.php*
A sassy mix of jazz from all points of
the European compass; movies, workshops and exhibitions too.

17 Mar **St Patrick's Day Parade
& Festival**
Across the city
www.stpatricksfestival.ie
The world's best excuse for a drink or
seven: the feast day of a Welshman who
ran the snakes out of Ireland. A five-day
festival of entertainment unravels.

April 2010

Early-mid April **Convergence
Festival**
Various venues
www.sustainable.ie/convergence
Conferences, theatre, film and more,
exploring ethical urban living.

May 2010

May **Dublin Dance Festival**
Various venues
www.dublindancefestival.ie
Innovative and often provocative
annual event that brings the best
international dance companies to
Dublin.

Festival fever

Analog p33

Dublin may have some of the most expensive concert tickets in Europe, but its reputation for passionate and loyal audiences is well earned, warranting over 70 festivals and outdoor shows between April and September in recent years.

When the **Electric Picnic** began in 2004 as a 'boutique' festival hoping to attract a mature audience away from the perennially sold-out **Oxegen**, few could have anticipated how quickly it would grow. Now a three-day 'music and arts' event with as many big-name acts as its rival, it has raised the standard for festivals in Ireland irreversibly. But for people who would rather do without tents and wellies, there's a host of festivals with inexpensive ticket prices and strong reputations.

New to the festival circuit is June's **Future Days**, which brings exciting, little-known indie bands to the city's smaller venues such as Whelan's and Vicar Street, a year or two before they appear at the mainstream festivals. Next, over three days in July, **Analog** does its bit for the Docklands regeneration, transforming Grand Canal Square into a hub for esoteric and forward-thinking acts such as Tortoise and the Cinematic Orchestra.

Drawing crowds in excess of 200,000 every August, Dún Laoghaire's **Festival of World Cultures** is easily the most diverse and family-friendly programme of all. If you can't find something among the workshops, circus and club nights, simply meander along the seafront through a village of gourmet food stalls until a parade of samba dancers sweeps you back towards some of the biggest names in world music.

September sees **Hard Working Class Heroes**, which brings together the best in emerging home-grown rock and pop talent. (There's plenty in the way of authentically Irish music and culture in the **Temple Bar TradFest** every January.) Finally, the **Dublin Electronic Arts Festival** (DEAF) celebrates cutting-edge electronic music and visual art across the city every October bank holiday weekend. Interested?

June 2010

June-Aug **Music in the Park**
Various venues
www.dublincity.ie
Laid-back jazz or rousing opera in the city's parks – and it's all free.

4-7 June **Docklands Maritime Festival**
Liffey Quays
www.dublindocklands.ie/maritimefestival
Tall ships on the Liffey, street theatre and a huge market for foodies.

7 June **Women's Mini-Marathon**
Fitzwilliam Square to St Stephen's Green
www.womensminimarathon.ie
The largest such event in the world. 30,000 runners (not all of them women) come to raise money for charity.

Mid June **Dublin Writers Festival**
Various venues
www.dublinwritersfestival.com
Top writers and poets from all over the world give readings, discussions and public debates; there's public slam too.

Mid June **Future Days**
Various venues
www.foggynotions.ie
Hip new rock bands. See box p35.

Mid June **Pride**
Various venues
www.dublinpride.org

A week-long gay festival: céilídh, drag contests, and the Pride march itself.

16 June **Bloomsday Festival**
James Joyce Centre
www.jamesjoyce.ie
A week of Joycean readings, performances, excursions and more.

July 2010

Ongoing Music in the Park

July-Aug **Jameson Movies on the Square**
Meeting House Square
www.templebar.ie
Cult and classic movies screened in the open air on Saturday nights.

Mid July **Dublin Circus Festival**
Various venues
www.templebar.ie
Roll up for a mix of performance art and traditional circus skills.

Mid July **Oxegen**
Punchestown Racecourse
www.oxegen.ie/www.mcd.ie
One of Ireland's only multi-stage rock festivals. See box p35.

Late July **Temple Bar's Chocolate Festival**
Various venues
www.templebar.ie
A festival in honour of the cocoa bean: films, carnival and choc workshop.

Fringe Festival p33

Itineraries

Blarney Woollen Mills p52

Traditional Dublin

It might be sandwiched between a branch of Karen Millen and a construction site, but traditional Dublin is still there if you look hard enough. Dream pubs, Georgian squares and poetic atmosphere await anyone prepared to look past the bland apartment blocks and painfully modern boutiques and restaurants that dot so many parts of the city.

A day exploring Dublin of old should start, nice and early, in **Bewley's Oriental Café** (p61) on Grafton Street. This Dublin institution is chaotic and noisy, but a cappuccino in such stain-glassed splendour makes it all worthwhile. When you've had your caffeine fix, turn right and walk to the top of Grafton Street, and cross the road

to the serenity of **St Stephen's Green** (p73). Walk around the formal gardens and willow fringed pond, looking at the various statues as you go, before leaving at the exit beside the Wolfe Tone memorial (known locally as Tonehenge).

Cross the road, looking at the gorgeous **Shelbourne Hotel** opposite (p143), and turn right down Merrion Row. After you pass the Huguenot Cemetery, turn left on to Merrion Street. You're now in the heart of Georgian Dublin – and the seat of Ireland's power. Merrion Square, Dublin's most prestigious address, is on your right, and the impressive **Leinster House** (p77), **National Museum of Archaeology** (p77) and **National Gallery** (p77) are on your left.

At the bottom of the road, turn left on to Clare Street, and left again on to Kildare Street, where you can see the WB Yeats exhibition at the **National Library** (p77). This permanent exhibition is free, and you only need pop in for a couple of minutes – just long enough to listen to the recording of WB reading his 'Lake Isle of Innisfree'.

Next, a spot of retail therapy at the **Blarney Woollen Mills** (p52) on Nassau Street. When you've loaded up with mohair rugs and pottery, cross the road to Trinity College, and walk through to the famous university quad. You'll see signs for the Book of Kells, but the queues are horrendous, so skip it and visit the beautiful **Old Library** (p50) instead. When you walk out on to College Green, the original Houses of Parliament are in front of you.

Battle up busy Dame Street for five minutes and you'll come to **Dublin Castle** (p59), where you'll find – albeit behind a car park – an oasis of calm and the cultural treasure that is the **Chester Beatty Library** (p55).

After all that culture, it's time for lunch, so cross Dame Street again to deli **Gruel** (p63) or its pricier sister restaurant, Mermaid. Both serve terrific Irish food, including beef stew and haddock chowder. When you're sated, cross back to the castle, where you're going to pick up the **Dublin Tourist Bus**. A ticket costs €15, but it's worth it: it's the only way to see all the sites in an afternoon, and its running commentary is surprisingly useful.

Ride the bus past **St Patrick's Cathedral** (p59) and **Christ Church Cathedral** (p58) and into the vibrant Liberties quarter – the home of the Guinness Brewery. If you're thirsty, hop off and visit the **Guinness Storehouse** (p116) for a pint of the black on the sixth-floor Gravity bar. Catch the next bus, getting off for the excellent tour of **Kilmainham Gaol** (p117): no other attraction gives you a better sense of Irish history. Catch another bus and ride past the grand Heuston Station and Phoenix Park, then get off for the **Dublin Writers' Museum** (p90) and **Hugh Lane Gallery** (p91). Both are well worth a visit – especially the gallery, for its reconstruction of Francis Bacon's studio.

From here, walk down Dublin's main thoroughfare, O'Connell Street. What it lacks in beauty it makes up for in history: it's home to Dublin's oldest hotel and department store – the **Gresham** (p144) and **Clery's** (p97) – as well as the **Gate** theatre (p101) and the bullet-ridden **GPO** (p90).

At the bottom of O'Connell Street, turn right on to Ormond Quay, where you'll find the small but perfectly formed **Winding Stair** bookshop (p98). Book a table at the Michelin-rated restaurant upstairs and enjoy an excellent, reasonably priced dinner overlooking the Liffey before heading to the pub. You could pick any one of a dozen boozers in the area, but we recommend the Stag's Head. To get here, cross the pretty Ha'penny Bridge and walk through Temple Bar to Dame Court.

After a pint here, float down Exchequer Street to the bottom of Grafton Street, where you should find a rickshaw which, for a few euros, will whisk you to Baggot Street for a live music session at **O'Donoghue's** (p82). *Sláinte*!

General Post Office p90

Dublin Zoo p102

Parkland Pleasures

This day-long walk takes you through the city's finest green spaces – starting with the biggest, and ending up at one of the smallest.

We begin at the vast expanse of **Phoenix Park** (p104), the largest city park in Europe. It contains an invigorating blend of formal gardens, casual meadows, sports fields and wild undergrowth, as well as – believe it or not – herds of deer. Inside the park is the official residence of the Irish president, Aras an Uachtarain, a Palladian lodge that was once the seat of the Lord Lieutenant of Ireland. Go in by the south-eastern entrance, where you'll see the formal People's Garden and across the road, the huge Wellington Monument.

A short stroll north-west of here takes you to the much-improved **Dublin Zoo** (p102). Opposite the zoo's main entrance is a lovely little wooden structure that serves excellent snacks. At the Phoenix Monument in the centre of the park, side roads and pathways will lead you to the **Visitors' Centre** (p104), the gracious 18th-century home of the American ambassador (not open to the public) and the towering Papal Cross, marking the spot where Pope John Paul II performed mass to the assembled multitudes during his 1979 visit.

Leave by the North Circular Road entrance (at the top of Infirmary Road), and catch the no.10 bus to O'Connell Street. Walk the short distance to Bloom's Lane and have lunch at **Bar Italia** (p91) or **Café Cagliostro** (p92).

Iveagh Gardens

Push on southwards along
Westmoreland Street and Grafton
Street, trying not to be distracted
by Trinity College or the many
shops on Grafton Street. You're
heading for **St Stephen's Green**
(p73), possibly the most famous
patch of grass in Dublin. But we're
interested in the beautiful gardens
and charmingly secluded spots
that cluster around it.

This exploration of the area's
leafy secrets begins with the often
overlooked **Iveagh Gardens**
(entrances on Hatch Street Upper
and Clonmel Street off Harcourt
Street). At first glance, the gardens
look private: they're ringed by high
stone walls and their entrances are
hidden. One door lurks behind the
National Concert Hall (p88) on
Earlsfort Terrace, another on
Clonmel Street; a few years ago, a
third gate was created on Hatch
Street, from which a flight of

concrete steps (flanked by a
wheelchair ramp) leads down to
the southernmost end of the circuit
of sequestered paths.

From here, turn left (leaving
the extraordinary mass of gnarled
tree roots behind you) and head
towards the gorgeous circular rose
garden. Stop to smell the flowers
before continuing on to the mini
maze (a pleasingly symmetrical
spectacle, and a welcome activity
for kids). From here, head north
through the trees into the open
section of the gardens, where two
imposing statue fountains face
each other across a sweep of
perfectly manicured lawn.
After the narrow paths and lichen-
covered statuary of the south side
of the gardens, the sense of space
here is exhilarating. Wander in
the direction of the northwest
corner and leave the gardens
on to Clonmel Street.

Turn right and head north up Harcourt Street, then take a left into Montague Street. This will lead you out on to Camden Street – the excellent **Bóbó's** burger bar (p79) will be enticing you from the other side of the road. Be strong, and walk past it into Camden Row, where, after a few paces, you'll come to the tiny St Kevin's Park squirrelled away to your right.

Formerly the graveyard of the ivy-strangled relic of a church at its centre, this beguiling little park is almost always empty. (Though rumour has it that the area is haunted by the restless souls whose gravestones have been pushed to the side of the now neatly tended lawns.) It's such a peaceful setting – a sensation heightened by the proximity of towering office blocks and busy roads – that St Kevin's can be one of the most relaxing places

in Dublin: immerse yourself in a book or sit on a bench and enjoy the twitter of birdsong.

But don't get too comfortable – there's one last hideaway to discover. Find your way back to where Camden Row joins Camden Street and turn right, heading south for a few hundred yards. This is prime student territory, with bars advertising happy hours, cafés touting cheap deals and copy shops with special rates on theses crowding the pavement. Stop at no.61, home to the high-quality paper company Daintree. Walk through the shop, past the shelves of speciality papers and bindings, and emerge at the back into the hidden courtyard of the **Cake Café** (p79). Sit down for a cup of something hot and a slice of something nice; you'll walk it off on the way back to town.

Dublin Against the Clock

Dublin is certainly a diminutive city, but with so many things to see and experience, you may find it hard to know where to begin. So, according to the amount of time you have at your disposal, choose one or more of our handy potted guides below.

A day in Dublin

If you only have 24 hours to spend in Dublin, you're going to have to get your skates on. To start with, get a feel for the atmosphere of the city with a wander around the lovely buildings, gardens and raucous playing fields of **Trinity College** (p48). You probably won't want to use up your time queuing for the **Book of Kells** (p50), but

you'd certainly do well to get a rush of blood to the brain at the on-campus **Science Gallery** (p51), which is much easier to get into. Now it's time for lunch at the **Lemon Crêpe & Coffee Company** (p64) or, for something much fancier, the **Town Bar and Grill** (p67). Afterwards, head down to Dame Street to see the glorious lobby of **City Hall** (p58), then make your way next door to **Dublin Castle** (p59). Don't feel obliged to pay to get inside the building; instead, wander through the Upper Yard to the free Dubh Linn Gardens and the **Chester Beatty Library** (p55).

Now your path leads northwards to the Liffey. Retrace your steps

National Museum of Archaeology and History p77

to City Hall, then walk along Parliament Street to the river. Stay on the southern bank for the time being, and turn right along Wellington Quay. The second bridge you come to is the famous Ha'penny Bridge, which spans the Liffey in an attractive shallow arch of white ironwork and is one of the city's best known landmarks. Cross it, turn immediately right along Bachelors Walk, until you get to the next bridge, O'Connell Bridge, which marks the start of O'Connell Street. This is Dublin's Champs-Elysées, home to the historic **GPO** (p90), the shiny new Spire and some excellent shops. If time allows, push on north to the **Dublin Writers' Museum** (p90); and then it's almost certainly time for dinner. Celebrate the city's growing cosmopolitanism with a meal at one of the nearby Chinese or Italian restaurants (see box p95); and finish off in classic Irish style at a Victorian pub – the **Patrick Conway** (p94).

Two days in Dublin

The pace for this larger-sized 'potted Dublin' is a little more leisurely. On the first day, follow the sequence laid out in the tour above. On day two, start by taking a walk down towards St Stephen's Green, the business hub of the city. Spend the morning shopping yourself silly on Grafton Street (remembering to pause for mid-morning refreshments in the famous old **Bewley's Oriental Café**; p61), drop into the **National Museum of Archaeology and History** (p77) for a look at some ancient Irish gold and lunch at one of Dublin's fancy restaurants (**Thornton's** is a good bet; p67).

Now it's time for a spot of culture. Compare and contrast the splendours of **St Patrick's Cathedral** (p59) and **Christ Church Cathedral** (p58), before fuelling up on buns and oodles of tea at **Cake Café** (p79).

Next, stroll back up O'Connell Street and lose yourself in the intricacies of Francis Bacon's studio inside the **Hugh Lane Gallery** (p91). Round the day off south of the river, in one of the better Temple Bar boozers – **Dakota** (p62), say, or the **Foggy Dew** (p63).

A week in Dublin

Having done all the above on your first few days, spread the net a little wider and spend a day exploring the wilds of **Phoenix Park** (p102) and **Dublin Zoo** (p102). Then, after a well-deserved kip, wake up fresh for a tour of Kilmainham and the Liberties, starting at the **Guinness Storehouse** (p116) and **Kilmainham Gaol** (p117), and ending up with a dose of cutting-edge creation at the **Irish Museum of Modern Art** (p116).

The next day, drift back into town and linger on the North Quays and in Temple Bar – seek out the corner cafés and quirky shops. Lunch at **Gruel** (p63) or **Fallon & Byrne** (p68) and take part in the daily rituals of Dubliners. Try, too, to devote a day to Docklands, the formerly atrophied limb of the city into which the life-blood of investment and bold design is now freely flowing.

Finally, having followed the advice above, you'll have had quite enough of city life, so rent a car and take a day trip to the glorious **Wicklow Mountains** (p132) or **Newgrange** (p132), where you can savour the mysteries of its palaeolithic burial mounds. If that sounds too energetic, hop on the DART to **Dalkey** (p123) for bracing sea walks followed by steaming plates of seafood or a pint in one of Dalkey's many lovely pubs.

Pedal taxis, O'Connell Street

Dublin by Area

Old Library p50

Trinity College & Around

There's a great atmosphere surrounding the sprawling, leafy campus of **Trinity College** – a pleasant blend of lofty academia (thanks to the grand buildings and statuary) and the vibrant traffic of students who move about the place in noisy gaggles or occupy the tree-shaded perimeters of the green, immersed in study or (more likely) lazy summer afternoon chats.

As you enter Front Square you'll see Sir William Chambers' neo-classical Chapel and Examination Hall. The Chapel interior – elegant, with a stuccoed ceiling – looks rather like a mini Houses of Parliament, with two rows of pews facing each other rather than the altar. The extremely pretty Campanile, designed by Charles Lanyon, rises up directly opposite the main portico, framing beautiful, ancient maple trees. During the summer, **Campus Tours** takes visitors around all the major on-campus sights.

The Museum Building, close by the **Old Library** was inspired by John Ruskin's celebration of Venetian Gothic and designed by Benjamin Woodward and Thomas Deane in 1852.

Although the elevation from Nassau Street doesn't look like much, it is worth making a detour to check out the exterior and atrium of the new Ussher Library, adjacent

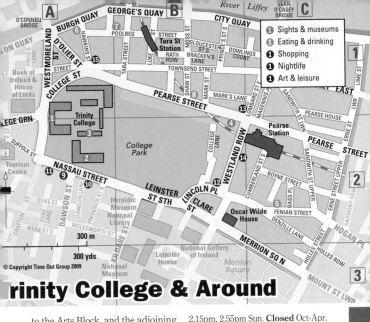

rinity College & Around

to the Arts Block, and the adjoining Berkeley Library, two fine examples of 1970s brutalism. Outside the Berkeley is Pomodoro's golden *Sphere within a Sphere*. The Pavilion (or 'Pav' to anyone who has ever set foot in the place), a drab enough building at the edge of the cricket pitch, comes into its own every summer by virtue of getting sun longer than almost anywhere else in the city. Gangs of students and former alumni mob the place, spilling out of the bar on to the steps and pitch.

Sights & museums

Campus Tours

Trinity College (896 1661/www.tcd.ie). All cross-city buses/Luas Abbey Street/ St Stephen's Green. **Open** *May-Sept Tours* 10.15am, 10.55am, 11.35am, 12.15pm, 12.55pm, 1.35pm, 2.15pm, 2.55pm, 3.40pm Mon-Sat; 10.15am, 10.55am, 11.35am, 12.15pm, 12.55pm, 2.15pm, 2.55pm Sun. **Closed** Oct-Apr. **Admission** €5; €10 (incl Old Library & Book of Kells). No credit cards. **Map** p49 A1 ❶

These student-led tours are not always very informative, but they are invariably enthusiastic, a fun sprint around the historical and architectural highlights of the campus. The tours last for half an hour and depart from a desk at the Front Arch of the College.

Douglas Hyde Gallery

Trinity College (896 1116/www.douglas hydegallery.com). All cross-city buses/ Luas Abbey Street/St Stephen's Green. **Open** 11am-6pm Mon-Wed, Fri; 11am-7pm Thur; 11am-4.45pm Sat. **Admission** free. **Map** p49 A2 ❷

This neat modernist exhibition space could scarcely be more at odds with the fusty, old-world atmosphere that Trinity tends to project to the outside world. The Douglas Hyde Gallery showcases the work of a wide variety of contemporary artists (recent shows

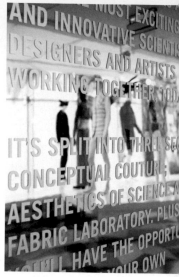

Science Gallery

have included exhibitions by Trisha Donnelly and Verne Dawson, with shows by such big names as Miroslav Tichy programmed for 2009). There are also occasional live music performances and art-house film screenings in the evening.

Old Library & Book of Kells

Trinity College (608 2308/www.tcd.ie/ library). All cross-city buses/Luas Abbey Street/St Stephen's Green. **Open** May-Sept 9.30am-5pm Mon-Sat; 9.30am-4.30pm Sun. Oct-Apr 9.30am-5pm Mon-Sat; noon-4.30pm Sun. **Admission** €8; €7 reductions; €16 family; free under-12s. **Map** p49 A2 ❸

'Kelly's Book', as it still gets called occasionally, is Trinity's most famous artefact, but it suffers slightly from *Mona Lisa* syndrome: it's so endlessly reproduced that it seems underwhelming in real life. The book, designed around the ninth century, is an illuminated copy of the Gospels in Latin, lovingly created by early Christian monks; at any one time four pages are on display – two illustrated and two text – inside a bullet-proof glass case. Alongside is the *Book of Durrow*, an even earlier illuminated manuscript of the Gospels, made in about 675.

There's also a multimedia exhibition to take you through the process of creating such texts – for diehard bibliophiles only – but most people just come to gawp at the texts. Each summer, an average of 3,000 people a day troop through the Old Library. The Long Room, a vaulted, echoing, dimly lit expanse that's best seen as empty as possible, is the city's most beautiful room: a perfect panelled chamber with rows of double-facing shelves holding about 200,000 lovingly bound old volumes, accessed by antique ladders and guarded by busts of literary giants (and, of course, by security guards). Running down the centre of the room is a spine of ten climate-controlled glass cases that display particularly rare or ancient volumes.

Science Gallery

NEW *Trinity College, Pearse Street (896 4091/www.sciencegallery.ie). All cross-city buses/Luas St Stephen's Green.* **Open** varies with programme. **Admission free. Map** p49 B2 ①

The newest and most innovative museum to open its doors on Trinity campus, the Science Gallery takes a fresh, fun and lively look at the applications of science across a number of walks of life. There's virtually nothing these people are not into: whether it's commissioning exhibitions of techno-thread clothing (togs that respond, think, even grow on their own) or 2008's superb Lightwave exhibition (back again in 2009) to displays of robotic art (that is, robots that are built to create art) and the series of Raw debates on subjects as diverse as the future of biofuels and the efficacy of anti-depressants. Basically, the Science Gallery is a fascinating, laudable new venture, and anyone with even a passing interest in science should take a look.

Eating & drinking

Ginger Man

40 Fenian Street (676 6388). All cross-city buses. **Open** 11am-12.30am Mon-Thur; 11am-1.30am Fri, Sat; 5-11pm Sun. **Pub. Map** p49 C2 ⑤

This small, old-fashioned pub is just round the corner from Merrion Square, and great for a pint or two after a jaunt around the museums. The regular pub quizzes are good fun, the atmosphere is always relaxed – and you can dine until 9pm if you choose.

Messrs Maguire

1-2 Burgh Quay (670 5777/www.messrsmaguire.ie). All cross-city buses/Luas Abbey Street. **Open** 10.30am-12.30am Mon, Tue; 10.30am-1.30am Wed; 10.30am-2am Thur; 10.30am-2.30am Fri, Sat; noon-midnight Sun. **Bar. Map** p49 A1 ⑥

This quayside spot tries really hard, but never quite seems to get there. Downstairs has dark flooring, wood stools and affable barmen, while upstairs there's more ambience –

despite the fact that it's obviously going for an old-school vibe. Still, it has its own microbrewery, so if you're tiring of the black stuff, you know where to make for.

Mulligan's

8 Poolbeg Street (677 5582/www. mulligans.ie). DART Tara Street. **Open** 10.30am-11.30pm Mon-Thur; 10.30am-12.30am Fri, Sat; 12.30-11pm Sun. **Pub**. **Map** p49 B1 **7**

This legendary Dublin boozer really comes into its own on a Sunday afternoon, when you can sit back and watch the Guinness settle. Mulligan's first opened its doors in 1782, and the tobacco-stained ceilings, glassy-eyed octogenarians and a no-mobiles policy mean it retains authenticity and is gloriously unpretentious. Things get seriously packed on weekday evenings as workers from nearby offices flood in for their daily jar.

O'Neill's

37 Pearse Street (671 4074). DART Pearse. **Open** noon-11.30pm Mon-Thur; noon-12.30am Fri, Sat. **Pub**. **Map** p49 B1 **8**

Pearse Street can feel a little quiet and desolate at night, but O'Neill's is one good reason to venture down this way. It's only a few minutes from College Green (but still well away from the crowds) and it's a fine bar in general, with lots of separate rooms and big glowing fires. The ventilation could be better. Gaggles of besuited folk drink here, but don't be put off: there are plenty of seats for all – and good pub grub too.

Shopping

Blarney Woollen Mills

21-23 Nassau Street (671 0068/ www.blarney.com). All cross-city buses/Luas St Stephen's Green. **Open** 9am-6pm Mon-Sat; 11am-6pm Sun. **Map** p49 A2 **9**

The main branch of this chain is actually located in the village of Blarney, so its name is not as shamelessly cheesy as all that. However, don't come here expecting the latest trends: what they stock is hand-woven items like throws, sweaters and scarves, plus souvenirs of the Waterford Crystal and Royal Tara china varieties.

Celtic Note

12 Nassau Street (670 4157/www. celticnote.com). All cross-city buses/Luas St Stephen's Green. **Open** 9am-7pm Mon-Wed, Fri, Sat; 9am-8pm Thur; 11am-6pm Sun. **Map** p49 A2 **10**

If you're after Irish stuff, this is the place to come (as you may have guessed from all those big posters of Glen Hansard and co in the window). Helpful staff are on hand to answer any queries, and the stock also includes a decent pick of British and American folk artists.

Design Yard

48 Nassau Street (474 1011/www. designyard.ie). All cross-city buses/ Luas St Stephen's Green. **Open** 10am-7pm Mon-Sat; 11am-6pm Sun. **Map** p49 A2 **11**

It may no longer be in its quaint Cow Lane location but Design Yard's high-end contemporary art and jewellery is looking as good as ever. Everything from beautiful rings and necklaces to limited-edition sculptures and ornate lamps is on sale here, alongside an interesting revolving programme of art exhibitions taking in subjects ranging from Dublin streetscapes to conflict diamonds.

Nightlife

Kennedy's

30-32 Westland Row (679 9077/www. theunderground.ie). All cross-city buses. **Open** 10am-11.30pm Mon-Thur, 10am-2.30am Fri, Sat. **Admission** prices vary. **Map** p49 B2 **12**

Thanks in part to resident electro/house DJs like Calvin James, Simon Hayes and Dave Salacious, new life has been breathed into this bar-cum-club venue. Given its proximity to Trinity College, expect a few students, but for the most part the crowd here is terminally trendy. The club night menu changes

Oisin Art Gallery p54

regularly, so best to consult listings to see who is playing. For the time being, this place is so hip it hurts.

Arts & leisure

Green on Red

26-28 Lombard Street East (671 3414/ www.greenonredgallery.com). All cross-city buses/Luas Busáras. **Open** 10am-6pm Mon-Fri; 11am-5pm Sat. **Map** p49 B1 ⑬

It may be a little off the beaten track, but this gallery on Lombard Street East is well worth seeking out, as many consider it to be one of the city's best. The high industrial ceiling complements the sparse contemporary works inside. The gallery represents some of the best local and international contemporary artists, including Mark Joyce, Gerard Byrne, Paul Doran, Alice Maher and Corban Walker.

Oisin Art Gallery

44 Westland Row (661 1315/ www.oisingallery.com). All cross-city buses/DART Pearse. **Open** 9am-5.30pm Mon-Fri; 10am-5.30pm Sat. **Map** p49 B2 ⑭

This central, popular gallery recently moved to a beautiful new space next door to its former home on Westland Row, and now it has more room; there's even a spacious courtyard. Oisin deals in traditional and contemporary artists, including Christine Bowen, John Skelton and Katy Simpson.

Screen

D'Olier Street (0818 300 301/www. omniplex.ie). All cross-city buses/Luas Abbey Street. **Open** 2-9pm daily. **Tickets** €7; €6-€8 reductions. **Map** p49 A1 ⑮

Just round the corner from Trinity College, the Screen is scuffed, tatty, eternally studenty, and its programme is exactly what you'd expect: offbeat without being obscure; a mix of second-run, limited-release, foreign-language and arthouse pictures that can pack them in at busy times. Two of the three screens have seats for couples, so take someone you'd like to know better.

Design Yard p52

Dublinia p59

Temple Bar & the Cathedrals

Temple Bar is Dublin's dynamo, an ever-buzzing hive of bold new facilities: music venues, funky hotels, boozers and free public Wi-Fi. But there's another side to it. The city's two great cathedrals (and, indeed, much of its religious heritage) also stand proudly within the margins of Temple Bar, a short walk – and yet a world away – from the stags and hens and the hordes of wining and dining tourists. It is, for the most part, a peaceful coexistence; in fact, it's thanks to this very dichotomy that Temple Bar is one of the most alluring (and the most visited) neighbourhood in Dublin.

Although the area can still be pretty unsavoury on weekend nights, it's one of the city's most charming spots in the day and early

evenings. The 18th-century cobbled streets make it ideal territory for the flâneur, with plenty of boutiques, galleries, bars, cafés and general architectural diversity. This is also where you'll find Grafton Street, Dublin's shopping heartland: an entire street is given over to the pursuit of retail therapy.

Sights & museums

Chester Beatty Library

Clock Tower Building, Dublin Castle, Dame Street (407 0750/www.cbl.ie). All cross-city buses/Luas Jervis/St Stephen's Green. **Open** *May-Sept* 10am-5pm Mon-Fri; 11am-5pm Sat; 1-5pm Sun. *Oct-Apr* 10am-5pm Tue-Fri; 11am-5pm Sat; 1-5pm Sun. *Guided tours* 1pm Wed; 3pm, 4pm Sun. **Admission** free. **Map** p56 C3 ❶

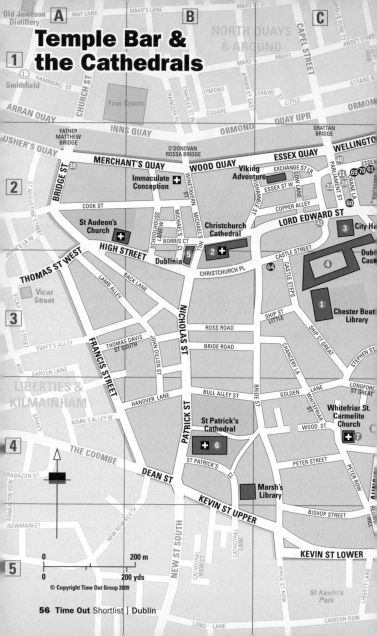

Temple Bar & the Cathedrals

A   **B**   **C**

Old Jameson Distillery

1

Smithfield

MAY LANE · MARY'S LANE · MARY ST LITTLE · WOLFE TONE ST · ABBEY ST · CAPEL STREET

NORTH QUAYS & AROUND

HAMMOND ST · CHURCH ST · MARY'S · ABBEY · ARRAN ST EAS · STRAND · STRAND S

ARRAN QUAY · ORMOND SQUARE · CHANCERY PL · CHARLES ST W

Four Courts

INNS QUAY · ORMOND · QUAY UPR · ORMOND

USHER'S QUAY

FATHER MATTHEW BRIDGE · O'DONOVAN ROSSA BRIDGE · GRATTAN BRIDGE · WELLINGTO

2

MERCHANT'S QUAY · WOOD QUAY · ESSEX QUAY

BRIDGE ST · 38 · Immaculate Conception · WINETAVERN ST · Viking Adventure · EXCHANGE ST LR · COW LANE · PARLIAMENT ST · 40 · 69 · 70 · 61 · ESSE · CRANE LA · 11 · 28 · 22 · 60

COOK ST · ESSEX ST W · COPPER ALLEY

ST AUGUSTINE ST · St Audeon's Church · SCHOOLHOUSE LANE · MICHAEL'S LANE · MICHAEL'S · Christchurch Cathedral · LORD EDWARD ST · 41 · City Ha

HIGH STREET · BORRIS CT · **5** · **2** · CASTLE STREET · **3** · Dubl Cas

JOHN'S LA W · Dublinia · HILL · CHRISTCHURCH PL · **4** · CASTLE STEPS

THOMAS ST WEST · BACK LANE · LAMB ALLEY · **1** · Chester Beat Library

Vicar Street · VICAR ST · SHIP ST LITTLE

3

THOMAS DAVIS ST SOUTH · ROSS ROAD · SHIP ST GREAT · STEPHEN S

SWIFT'S ALLEY · JOHN DILLON ST · BRIDE ROAD · CHANCERY LA

ASH ST · GARDEN LANE · NICHOLAS ST · GOLDEN LANE · LONGFOR

LIBERTIES & KILMAINHAM · FRANCIS STREET · HANOVER LANE · BULL ALLEY ST · BRIDE ST · WHITEFRIAR ST · Whitefriar St. Carmelite Church · **7**

MARK'S ALLEY W · PATRICK ST · WOOD ST · PETER ROW

4

BRABAZON ST · THE COOMBE · St Patrick's Cathedral · **6** · PETER STREET

NEW ROW SOUTH · DEAN ST · ST PATRICK'S CL · ST PATRICK'S · Marsh's Library · BISHOP STREET

NEWMARKET · KEVIN ST UPPER · KEVIN ST LOWER

5

0   200 m
0   200 yds

© Copyright Time Out Group 2009

NEW ST SOUTH · CATHEDRAL LANE · CATHEDRAL VIEW CT · BRIDE ST NEW · St Kevin's Park · LIBERTY LANE

LONG LANE · CAMDEN ROW

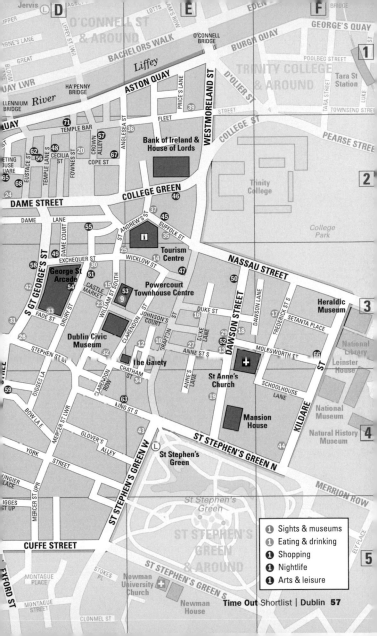

Chester Beatty Library p55

Many of the best items from Sir Alfred Chester Beatty's priceless art collection are housed in this purpose-built museum: Buddhas, Chinese lanterns, snuff boxes, Japanese woodcuts, and some of the earliest Christian scrolls. If you tire of religious artefacts, the collection of illustrated 20th-century texts includes a storybook by Matisse and charming 1920s Paris fashion plates. Upstairs is a Zen roof garden; on the ground floor is the pleasantly tranquil Silk Road café and a well-stocked museum shop.

Christ Church Cathedral

Christ Church Place (677 8099/www. cccdub.ie). Bus 49, 50, 54A, 56A, 65, 77, 77A, 78A, 123/Luas Four Courts. **Open** *June-Aug* 9am-6pm daily. *Sept-May* 9.45am-5pm daily. **Admission** €6; €4 reductions.
Map p56 B2 ❷

Dubliners chiefly know Christ Church as home to the bells that ring out on New Year's Eve ('the largest full-circle ringing peal in the world') and for its choral evensong (Wednesdays and Thursdays at 6pm, Saturdays at 5pm, Sundays at 3.30pm). The building dates from the 1180s, and is handsome rather than spectacular. Look out for the heart-shaped iron box said to contain the heart of St Laurence O'Toole, and for the mummified cat and rat – supposedly found in an organ pipe and displayed in mid chase, like a frame from a Tex Avery cartoon.

City Hall

Dame Street (222 2204/www.dublin city.ie). All cross-city buses/Luas Jervis. **Open** 10am-5.15pm Mon-Sat; 2-5pm Sun. **Admission** €4; €2 reductions; €10 family. **Map** p56 C2 ❸

City Hall certainly has grandeur. Enter by the main Dame Street portico and you find yourself in Thomas Cooley's domed atrium, with its mosaic floor, sweeping staircases, frescoes by James Ward showing scenes from the history of Dublin, and four marble statues, one of which is Daniel O'Connell. In the basement is the Story of the Capital, an exhibition on the city's history of government, and a tiny café.

Dublin Castle

Dame Street (677 7129/www.dublin castle.ie). All cross-city buses/Luas Jervis/St Stephen's Green. **Open** (guided tour only) 10am-4.45pm Mon-Fri; 2-4.45pm Sat, Sun. **Admission** €4.50; €2-€3.50 reductions. No credit cards. **Map** p56 C3 ❹

Formerly the seat of British power in Ireland, this is less a castle than a set of 18th-century administrative buildings, albeit very fine ones. Its role is to host diplomatic or state functions, and occasional arts events such as recitals. The interior, including the lovely State Rooms, is visible by guided tour only.

Dublinia

Christ Church, St Michael's Hill (679 4611/www.dublinia.ie). Bus 49, 50, 51B, 54A, 56A, 65, 77, 77A, 78A, 123/Luas Four Courts. **Open** Apr-Sept 10am-5pm daily (doors close 4.15pm). Oct-Mar 11am-4pm Mon-Fri (doors close 3.15pm); 10am-4pm Sat, Sun (doors close 3.15pm). **Admission** €6.25; €3.75-€5.25 reductions; €17 family. **Map** p56 B3 ❺

Overall this exhibition is the best of its kind in Dublin. A scale model of the medieval city puts the two cathedrals in their geographical context, and there's a reconstructed archaeological dig. St Michael's Tower provides a fine view of the heart of old Dublin.

St Patrick's Cathedral

St Patrick's Close (453 9472/www.st patrickscathedral.ie). Bus 49X, 50, 50X, 54A, 56A, 77X, 150/Luas St Stephen's Green. **Open** Mar-Oct 9am-6pm Mon-Sat; 9-11am, 12.45-3pm, 4.15-6pm Sun. Nov-Feb 9am-6pm Mon-Fri; 9am-5pm Sat; 10-11am, 12.45-3pm Sun. **Admission** €5.50; €4.20 reductions; €15 family. **Map** p56 B4 ❻

This, the largest church in Ireland, dates from the 13th century, but was set on a far older site associated with St Patrick. Its plaques and monuments commemorate celebrated Anglican figures, from Richard Boyle (Earl of Cork and 'father of chemistry') to presidents of Ireland such as Erskine Childers; and also honour thousands of Irishmen who

fought and lost their lives for the British Empire. But St Patrick's is most famous for its association with the satirist Jonathan Swift, who wrote his best-known works while he was dean here from 1713 to 1745. He's buried here alongside his partner and friend, Stella.

A pleasant (and surprisingly large) green expanse adjoins the cathedral. At the eastern edge of the park are several plaques commemorating Ireland's brightest literary stars.

Whitefriar Street Carmelite Church

Whitefriar Street, off Aungier Street (475 8821/www.carmelites.ie). Bus 16, 16A, 19, 19A, 83, 122/Luas St Stephen's Green. **Open** 7.30am-6pm Mon, Wed-Fri; 7.30am-9pm Tue; 8.30am-7pm Sat; 7.30am-7pm Sun. **Admission** free. **Map** p56 C4 ❼

The altar of this Byzantine-looking church is said to contain the relics of St Valentine, and so has a busy season in February; another treasure is Our Lady of Dublin, a beautiful medieval wooden statue of the Virgin. At the back of the building is a very pretty garden with rose bushes and one little bench.

Eating & drinking

Bald Barista

NEW *68 Aungier Street (475 8616). All cross-city buses/Luas St Stephen's Green.* **Open** 6.30am-6pm daily. **Café**. **Map** p56 C4 ❽

The barista is Buzz Fendall, a man on a mission to 'bring amazing coffee to Dublin' – a mission accomplished on a daily basis at this busy, friendly café. Beans are bought from farmers in Brazil, Sumatra and Ethiopia, and freshly ground on site; food is served on the mezzanine or the small terrace. The best coffee in Dublin.

Ba Mizu

Powerscourt Townhouse Centre, 59 William Street South (674 6712/www. bamizu.com). All cross-city buses. **Open** noon-11.30pm Mon-Wed; noon-2.30am Thur-Sat; 12.30-11pm Sun. **Bar**. **Map** p57 D3 ❾

Queen Of Tarts

"Queen of tarts 'must be' one of the treats experienced when you visit Dublin". New York Times.

Pastry Shop & Cafe

Cow's Lane, Temple Bar.
Tel: 01 6334681

Also Dame Street, Dublin 2.
Tel: 01 6707499

www.queenoftarts.ie

Monday - Friday	7.30 am - 7 pm
Weekend	9 am - 7pm

Whitefriar Street Carmelite Church p59

Richly decorated in dark wood and odd art, Ba Mizu is one of Dublin's better upmarket watering holes. Soft lighting and plush leather armchairs make the lobby bar perfect for a nocturnal rendezvous; the back bar is brighter and busier. Look underfoot and you'll see a river running through the bar.

Bewley's Oriental Café

78 Grafton Street (672 7720/www. bewleys.ie/www.bewleyscafetheatre.com). All cross-city buses/Luas St Stephen's Green. **Open** 8am-10pm Mon-Wed; 8am-11pm Thur-Sat; 9am-10pm Sun. **Café. Map** p57 E3 ⑩

This famous Dublin address has quite a pedigree. Ernest Bewley opened the first of his Oriental Cafés over a century ago, and this flagship café opened in 1927. It's now the only one bearing the Bewley's name, and worth visiting – if only to breakfast by the original Harry Clarke windows on the ground floor. No.78 is also home to Bewley's Café Theatre, Dublin's only year-round venue for lunchtime drama; it puts on jazz and comedy in the evenings.

Brick Alley Café

25 East Essex Street, Temple Bar (679 3393). All cross-city buses/Luas Jervis.

Open 9am-10.30pm Mon-Wed; 9am-11pm Thur, Fri; 9am-midnight Sat; 10am-10pm Sun. No credit cards. **Café. Map** p56 C2 ⑪

This delightful café is small and often crowded, but a tasty menu and excellent coffee make up for it. The food – lots of sarnies, and specials like Irish stew or lasagne – is good and filling.

Bruxelles

7-8 Harry Street, off Grafton Street (677 5362). All cross-city buses/Luas St Stephen's Green. **Open** 10.30am-1.30am Mon-Wed; 10.30am-2.30am Thur-Sat; noon-1.30am Sun. **Bar. Map** p57 E3 ⑫

One of those Dublin institutions that somehow appeals to almost everyone – hairy, heavy metal fans, indie kids, codgers, students and tourists. The rockers and mods bars downstairs play weird tunes; upstairs is for a good pint and a chat. It needs a lick of paint, but the place has pots of charm.

Carluccio's

NEW *52 Dawson Street (633 3957/ www.carluccios.com). All cross-city buses/Luas St Stephen's Green.* **Open** 7am-10pm Mon-Fri; 8am-10.30pm Sat; 9am-10pm Sun. **Café. Map** p57 E3 ⑬

DUBLIN BY AREA

Bald Barista p59

The Carluccio's formula – good, affordable Italian food – is well known; and the first branch to open outside England is a corker. A small but well stocked deli acts as a foyer to the smart, two-tier café, where you can get anything from seductive coffee and cakes to pasta (tortellini filled with venison) and mains (chargrilled lamb chops with peppers).

Cornucopia

19 Wicklow Street (677 7583). All cross city buses/Luas St Stephen's Green. **Open** 8.30am-8pm Mon-Wed, Fri, Sat; 9am-9pm Thur; noon-7pm Sun. **€. Vegetarian**. **Map** p57 E3 ⑭

A stalwart for vegetarians, vegans, dairy intolerants or anyone looking for healthy, wholesome grub, Cornucopia is cramped and not exactly glam. Still, you'll be so thrilled with yourself after eating lentils, hearty soups and salads that you won't mind. For best results, come mid morning, when the atmosphere is at its most relaxed.

Dakota

9 William Street South (672 7696/www. dakota bar.ie). All cross-city buses/Luas St Stephen's Green. **Open** noon-11.30pm Mon-Wed, Sun; noon-2am Thur; noon-2.30am Fri, Sat. **Bar**. **Map** p57 D3 ⑮

Dim lighting and leather booths make Dakota one of Dublin's coolest and busiest late-night bars. It's a great place for a sociable drink and quiet during the day; it also does excellent mixed platters of finger food.

Davy Byrnes

21 Duke Street (677 5217/www.davy byrnes.com). All cross-city buses/Luas St Stephen's Green. **Open** 11am-11.30pm Mon-Wed; 11am-12.30am Thur, Fri; 10.30am-12.30am Sat; 12.30am-11pm Sun. **Pub**. **Map** p57 E3 ⑯

In *Ulysses*, Leopold Bloom stops here for a gorgonzola sandwich and a glass of burgundy; the bar is now a regular for well-dressed Dubliners. Seating can be scarce, and the place is better suited to conversation than revelry. The food – more fish and chips than gorgonzola and burgundy – is quite good.

Dunne & Crescenzi

14-16 Frederick Street South (671 9135/www.dunneandcrescenzi.com).

*All cross-city buses/Luas St Stephen's
Green.* **Open** 7.30am-11pm Mon-Sat;
10am-10pm Sun. **Café**. Map p57 F3 ⑰
D & C is probably the best Italian café
in town – or, more accurately, Italian
cafés: it occupies two adjoining
spaces, both small, dark and busy.
The food is wonderful: the tasty, fresh
and simple lunches include cured and
smoked meats, salads and panini;
there's also a full wine list and, natch,
fantastic coffee.

Farm

NEW *3 Dawson Street (671 8654).
All cross-city buses/Luas St Stephen's
Green.* **Open** 11am-11pm daily. **€€**.
International. Map p57 E3 ⑱
This fresh and funky restaurant caters
for two types of diner. Good ingredients are put to imaginative use in its
vegetarian dishes, from Asian green
salads to tasty tarts; meat-eaters get to
bite juicy steaks, burgers and grills.
Pizzas are made with organic dough,
and the kids' menu has health-con-
scious versions of classic junior hits
such as organic chicken nuggets. Lime-
green banquettes and table decorations
in flowerpots complete the picture.

Fitzers

*50 Dawson Street (677 1155/www.
fitzers.ie). All cross-city buses/Luas St
Stephen's Green.* **Open** 11.30am-11pm
Mon-Thur, Sun; 11.30am-11.30pm Fri,
Sat. **€€**. **International**.
Map p57 E4 ⑲
This popular branch of the small
family-run Fitzers chain is a good bet
for a 'between museums' break, or even
for a low-key dinner out with friends.
The menu includes dishes like grilled
sea bass with shaved fennel or
spaghetti tossed with feta, rocket, olives
and tomatoes. It's a professional, pleasant and consistently busy operation.

Foggy Dew

*1 Fownes Street Upper (677 9328).
All cross-city buses/Luas Jervis.* **Open**
noon-11.30pm Mon, Tue; 11am-12.30am
Wed; 11am-1am Thur; 11am-2am Fri,
Sat; 1pm-1am Sun. No credit cards.
Pub. Map p57 D2 ⑳

Named after an Irish ballad, this is one
of the few Temple Bar pubs that pulls
in a healthy mix of tourists and locals.
Indeed, since its refurbishment, it has
pulled in the same jokers who once
dubbed it the 'Dodgy Few'. It hosts the
best of Irish and international alternative music; get here early and lay claim
to one of the charming snugs.

Les Frères Jacques

*74 Dame Street (679 4555/www.les
freresjacques.com). All cross-city
buses/Luas Jervis.* **Open** 12.30-2.30pm,
7-10.30pm Mon-Thur; 12.30-2.30pm,
7-11pm Fri; 7-11pm Sat. **€€€**.
French. Map p56 C2 ㉑
Its many fans don't mind its location
on this grotty street, nor its cramped
interior: they concentrate instead on
Les Frères' spanking fresh seafood,
game in season, excellent cheese plates
and delicious home-made tarts. One of
Dublin's top French restaurants.

Front Lounge

*33-34 Parliament Street (670 4112).
All cross-city buses.* **Open** noon-
11.30pm Mon, Wed, Thur; noon-1am
Tue; noon-2am Fri; 3pm-2am Sat;
3-11.30pm Sun. **Bar**. Map p56 C2 ㉒
A good distance from the madding
crowds, this place has a relaxed atmosphere for refined drinking: velvet
couches, black marble tables and lots
of beautiful people. The Back Lounge
to the rear is a gay fave.

Grogan's Castle Lounge

*15 William Street South (677 9320).
All cross-city buses/Luas St Stephen's
Green.* **Open** 10.30am-11.30pm Mon-
Thur; 10.30am-12.30am Fri, Sat;
12.30-11pm Sun. No credit cards.
Pub. Map p57 D3 ㉓
Grogan's has a relaxed, shabby charm,
great Guinness and tasty toasted sandwiches. The sometimes bizarre art on
the walls is for sale, often put there by
punters. A Dublin drinking institution.

Gruel

*68A Dame Street (670 7119). All
cross-city buses/Luas Jervis.* **Open** 9am-
10pm Mon-Fri; 11am-10.30pm Sat, Sun.
No credit cards. **Café**. Map p57 D2 ㉔

Gruel's tasty, belly-filling bonanzas include hot roast in a roll (weekdays), hearty brunches (weekends), huge soups, pizza and home-made cakes, all at bargain prices. Its grown-up sister Mermaid is next door.

International Bar

23 Wicklow Street (677 9250). All cross-city buses/Luas St Stephen's Green. **Open** 10.30am-11.30pm Mon-Thur; 10.30am-12.30am Fri, Sat; 12.30-11pm Sun. No credit cards. **Bar**. Map p57 D3 ㉕
The laid-back International's long bar is always lined with Guinness-drinking regulars. An interesting crowd spills out on to the street in fine weather to sit and swap stories. There are also regular comedy nights.

Jaipur

41 South Great George's Street (677 0979 www.jaipur.ie). All cross-city buses/Luas St Stephen's Green. **Open** 5-11pm daily. **€€**. **Indian**. Map p57 D3 ㉖
Jaipur is a top-notch Indian, with branches on all three sides of the city. Service is very courteous, and food is light and tasty, including excellent fish and seafood options – a rich Goan seafood curry, say, or sea bass steamed with curry leaves.

Kehoe's

9 South Anne Street (677 8312). All cross-city buses/Luas St Stephen's Green. **Open** 10.30am-11.30pm Mon-Thur; 10.30am-12.30am Fri, Sat; 12.30-11pm Sun. **Pub**. Map p57 E3 ㉗
Its tiny loo aside, Kehoe's is rich with old-style character and snugs. Friendly staff serve creamy Guinness, and the upstairs bar has changed little since John Kehoe died many years ago.

Larder

8 Parliament Street (633 3581). All cross-city buses/Luas Jervis. **Open** 7.30am-6pm Mon, Tue; 7.30am-11pm Wed-Fri; 9am-11pm Sat, Sun. **Café**. Map p56 C2 ㉘
Larder is a prince among cafés. The food is a cut above normal café fare – Moroccan meatballs with mint-scented

couscous, say – and there are plenty of great wines (as well as excellent smoothies, great teas and Illy coffee) and plenty of space in the long dining room. Try to grab the wing-backed armchairs right in the window.

Lemon Crêpe & Coffee Company

60 Dawson Street (672 8898/www. lemonco.com). All cross-city buses/Luas St Stephen's Green. **Open** 8am-7.30pm Mon-Wed, Fri; 8am-9pm Thur; 9am-7.30pm Sat; 10am-6.30pm Sun. No credit cards. **Café**. Map p57 E3 ㉙
With its yellow walls and citrus-burst mural, this crêpe specialist certainly lives up to its name. Sweet and savoury pancake snacks hit the spot (the Nutella, ice-cream and strawberry version is heavenly), and if you want a sandwich or omelette, they can do that too. The café is small and crowded, so you might prefer a table outside – a good spot for a tasty morning coffee.

Léon

33 Exchequer Street (670 7238/www. cafeleon.ie). All cross-city buses/Luas St Stephen's Green/Jervis. **Open** 8am-10pm Mon-Wed, Thur; 8am-11pm Fri, Sat; 10am-10pm Sun. **Café**. Map p57 D3 ㉚
Part of a trinity of excellent cafés in Temple Bar, this branch of Léon has a charming old-world atmosphere (parquet floor, mismatched chairs, chandelier) and is a popular spot for first-class coffee and heavenly pastries; after noon a more elaborate French bistro menu kicks in. This is Dublin's version of Left Bank café society.

Long Hall

51 South Great George's Street (475 1590). All cross-city buses/Luas St Stephen's Green. **Open** 4-11.30pm Mon-Wed, Sun; 1-11.30pm Thur; 1pm-12.30am Fri, Sat; 1-11pm Sun. No credit cards. **Pub**. Map p57 D3 ㉛
This ornate Victorian gin palace has it all: jovial barman, characterful regulars, antique chandeliers and mirrored bar. Still regarded as one of Dublin's unmissable boozers.

Larder

Mao

*Chatham Row (670 4899/www.cafe
mao.com). All cross city buses/Luas St
Stephen's Green.* **Open** noon-10pm
Mon, Tue; noon-11pm Wed-Sat; 1.30-
9pm Sun. **€€**. **Asian**. Map p57 D3 ③②
Two floors in bold primary colours,
generous portions of pan-Asian grub
and a good location make this outlet of
the Mao mini chain a hit. You can get
everything from satay and wontons to
nasi goreng and chilli plum duck;
there's wine and beer, as well as juices
and soft drinks. The yoghurt, honey
and banana lassi is very moreish.

Market Bar

*Fade Street, off South Great George's
Street (613 9094/www.marketbar.ie).
All cross-city buses/Luas St Stephen's
Green.* **Open** noon-11.30pm Mon-Thur;
noon-12.30am Fri, Sat; 4-11pm Sun.
Bar. **Map** p57 D3 ③③
The Market Bar was once a pig
abattoir; it's now one of the city's most
popular bars. There's a no-music
policy, so noisy chatter wafts through

the lofty space. The tapas menu is good
value and well worth sampling.

Neary's

*1 Chatham Street (677 8596). All
cross-city buses/Luas St Stephen's
Green.* **Open** 10.30am-11.30pm Mon-
Thur; 10.30am-12.30am Fri, Sat; 12.30
11pm Sun. **Bar**. Map p57 E4 ③④
Mahogany, plush seating and heavy
curtains give Neary's a unique atmosphere. The friendly barmen serve an
excellent pint of plain; upstairs is an
elegant cocktail lounge with perhaps
the politest staff in Dublin.

Nude

*21 Suffolk Street (677 4804/www.
nude.ie). All cross-city buses/Luas St
Stephen's Green.* **Open** 7.30am-9pm
Mon-Wed; 7.30am-10pm Thur; 8am-
9pm Sat; 9am-8pm Sun. **Café**.
Map p57 E2 ③⑤
The glass roof and the wood-clad walls
create an outdoorsy vibe at this busy
outlet of the virtuous Dublin chain.
Nude specialises in food that tastes
good and does you good: freshly

DUBLIN BY AREA

Lemon Crêpe & Coffee Company p64

squeezed juices, superbly hearty 'bread bowl stews', wraps and salads (the chick-pea and chilli is a good one).

Oliver St John Gogarty

58-59 Fleet Street (671 1822/www. gogartys.ie). All cross-city buses. **Open** *Bar* 10.30am-2am Mon-Thur; 10.30am-2.30am Fri, Sat; 10.30am-1am Sun. *Lounge* 6pm-2.30am Mon-Thur; 3pm-2.30am Fri- Sun. **Bar**. **Map** p57 E2
Named after the man parodied as Buck Mulligan in *Ulysses*, this place got its bar counter from the green room in the Theatre Royal. Bands play traditional music nightly, and the seafood in the upstairs restaurant is very good.

O'Neill's

2 Suffolk Street (679 3671/www.oneills bar.com). All cross-city buses. **Open** 10.30am-11.30pm Mon-Thur; 10.30am-12.30am Fri, Sat; noon-11pm Sun. **Bar**. **Map** p57 E2 ③
O'Neills is labyrinthine and chaotic, but there are enough pleasant nooks to make it a cosy spot, despite its substantial size. The meat-and-two-veg lunch from the carvery is highly regarded by drinkers looking for soakage.

O'Shea's Merchant

12 Bridge Street Lower (679 3797). Bus 21, 21A/Luas Four Courts. **Open** 10.30am-11.30pm Mon-Wed; 10.30am-2am Thur-Sat; 12.30pm-2am Sun. **Map** p56 A2 ③
A taste of life beyond the Pale: Irish dancing, traditional Irish music, Gaelic football and hurling on the telly, decent Irish food, and intriguing Irish 'country nights' on Wednesdays.

Palace

21 Fleet Street (bar 677 9290/lounge 679 3037/www.palacebar.com). All cross-city buses/Luas Abbey Street. **Open** *Bar* 10.30am-11.30pm Mon-Thur; 10.30am-12.30am Fri, Sat; 12.30-11pm Sun. *Lounge* 7-11.30pm Tue; 5-11.30pm Wed, Thur; 5pm-12.30am Fri; 6.30pm-12.30am Sat; 6-11pm Sun. **Bar**. **Map** p57 E1 ③
The oldest bar in Dublin to have kept its original form – aged marble counter, mirrored alcoves – the grand old Palace deserves a place on any pub crawl, and has good literary cachet.

Porterhouse

16-18 Parliament Street (679 8847/ www.porterhousebrewco.com).

All cross-city buses/Luas Jervis. **Open**
11.30am-11.30pm Mon-Wed; 11.30am-
2am Thur; 11.30am-2.30am Fri; noon-
2.30am Sat; 12.30-11pm Sun. **Pub**.
Map p56 C2 ⑩
Dublin's oldest microbrewery pub
sprawls over three storeys. Its
decor may be rustic, but its stouts,
lagers and ales are better than any
mass-produced beer; the Oyster Stout,
made on the premises with real oysters, is truly superb. It also serves fine,
affordable pub food.

Queen of Tarts

4 Cork Hill, Dame Street (670 7499).
All cross-city buses. **Open** 7.30am-7pm
Mon-Fri; 9am-7pm Sat, Sun. No credit
cards. **Café. Map** p56 C2 ⑪
The Queen of Tarts has extended its
sovereignty with a large new branch
just around the corner. Breakfasts
might be potato cakes or scones with
raspberries; the lunchtime savoury
tarts are light, flaky and delicious; and
everything is baked here. There's also
a wide range of cakes and puddings.

Sixty6

66 South Great George's Street (400
5878/www.brasseriesixty6.com). All
cross-city buses/Luas St Stephen's
Green. **Open** 8am-3pm, 5-11pm Mon-
Thur; 10am-11.30pm Fri, Sat, 10am-
11pm Sun. **€€€. Brasserie**.
Map p57 D3 ⑫
Sixty6 is a stylish, easygoing brasserie
with loads of original touches (like the
antique china plates on the walls). The
menu has a knack for hitting just the
right note: devilled chicken livers on
rye toast to start, say, followed by duck
breast stuffed with apricot and prunes.
It even does breakfast.

Thornton's

Fitzwilliam Hotel, St Stephen's Green
West (478 7008/fitzwilliamhotel.com).
All cross-city buses/Luas St Stephen's
Green. **Open** 7-10pm Tue, Wed; noon-
2.30pm, 7-10pm Thur-Sat. **€€€€**.
Haute cuisine. Map p57 E4 ⑬
This much talked-about fine-dining
restaurants is run by TV chef Kevin
Thornton. Come here to experience his
exquisitely refined seasonal cooking:

perhaps mallard duck crusted with pistachio and honey, with a nettle and
thyme sorbet to cleanse the palate. Or,
if you'd prefer not to know what you'll
be eating, plump for the 'surprise
menu', a spread of eight unannounced
courses served at the 'chef's table'.

Town Bar and Grill

21 Kildare Street (662 4724/www.town
barandgrill.ie) All cross-city buses/
Luas St Stephen's Green. **Open** 12.30-
11pm Mon- Sat; 12.30-10pm Sun. **€€€**.
International. Map p57 F4 ⑭
This fashionable basement dining
room has a wealthy feel, and although
the kitchen has a soft spot for Italian
ingredients, the menu is largely international: white asparagus and arti-
choke with a soft-boiled egg and
shaved pecorino is a typical starter; yellow fin tuna and corn-fed chicken are
among the mains. The good wine list
has a strong showing of Tuscan reds.

Shopping

Avoca

11-13 Suffolk Street (677 4215/
www.avoca.ie). **All cross-city buses/**
Luas St Stephen's Green. **Open** 10am-
6pm Mon-Wed, Fri; 10am-8pm Thur;
10am-6.30pm Sat; 11am-6pm Sun.
Map p57 E2 ⑮
Avoca is often busy, but it's worth
braving the crowds. As well as a good
selection of clothing, the three-floor
store bursts at the seams with pretty
jewellery, unusual gifts, cute children's clothing and a good selection of
non-fiction books. Downstairs you'll
find a modern, casual café and deli
selling delectable breads and a tempting array of cakes.

Books Upstairs

36 College Green (679 6687/www.books
irish.com). All cross-city buses/Luas St
Stephen's Green. **Open** 10am-7pm
Mon-Fri; 10am-6pm Sat; 1-6pm Sun.
Map p57 E2 ⑯
This independent bookshop has been
going for decades. It has a fine stock of
Irish lit, and good drama, philosophy,
psychology, history and gay sections.

Brown Thomas

88-95 Grafton Street (605 6666/www.
brownthomas.com). All cross-city buses/
Luas St Stephen's Green. **Open** 9am-
8pm Mon, Wed, Fri; 9.30am-8pm Tue;
9am-9pm Thur; 9am-7pm Sat; 11am-
7pm Sun. **Map** p57 E3 ❹

BT is plush and painfully fashionable:
it has more designer labels than you
could shake a stick of celery at, not to
mention a personal shopping service, a
Vera Wang bridal salon and more.

Claddagh Records

2 Cecilia Street (677 0262/www.
claddaghrecords.com). All cross-city
buses/Luas Abbey Street. **Open**
10.30am-5.30pm Mon-Fri; noon-5.30pm
Sat. **Map** p57 D2 ❽

Traditionalists will love Claddagh's
extensive stock of Irish folk tunes –
everything here from early trad record-
ings to the most recent releases.

Fallon & Byrne

Exchequer Building, 11-17 Exchequer
Street (472 1010/www.fallonandbyrne.
com). All cross-city buses/Luas Jervis/
St Stephen's Green. **Open** 8am-10pm
Mon-Fri; 9am-9pm Sat; 11am-8pm Sun.
Map p57 D3 ❾

The city's top food shop, with a warehouse vibe and high shelves laden with
luxury deli items. Buy a delicious sarnie
and top-notch coffee at the café counter;
or try the pleasant, efficient restaurant
serving refined brasserie fare – roast
saddle of pancetta-wrapped rabbit
stuffed with wild mushroom mousse,
for example – and a good wine cellar.

Hodges Figgis

56-58 Dawson Street (677 4754).
All cross-city buses/Luas St Stephen's
Green. **Open** 9am-7pm Mon-Wed, Fri;
9am-8pm Thur; 9am-6pm Sat; noon-
6pm Sun. **Map** p57 E3 ❺

Wall-to-wall books over three tightly
packed floors, and a good selection of
special offers on throughout the year.

Jenny Vander

50 Drury Street (677 0406). All cross-
city buses/Luas St Stephen's Green.
Open 10.30am-5.30pm Mon-Sat.
Map p57 D3 ❺

This exquisite vintage clothing store
carries an elegant range of carefully
selected threads, hats, shoes and accessories. The range of designer antique
jewellery is particularly impressive.

Louis Mulcahy

46 Dawson Street (670 9311/www.louis
mulcahy.com). All cross-city buses/Luas
St Stephen's Green. **Open** 10am-6pm
Mon-Wed, Fri, Sat; 10am-8pm Thur.
Map p57 E3 ❺

You can't fit one of Mulcahy's vases
into your suitcase, but there's plenty of
smaller stuff that you can: attractive
stoneware and the new Dearg line.

Powerscourt
Townhouse Centre

59 William Street South (671 7000/
www.powerscourtcentre.com). All cross-
city buses/Luas St Stephen's Green.
Open 10am-6pm Mon-Wed, Fri, Sat;
10am-8pm Thur; noon-6pm Sun.
Map p57 D3 ❺

A remarkably calm, quiet and elegant
spot, with impressive plasterwork,
exposed brickwork and an imposing
staircase, this is one of the city's best
18th-century Georgian buildings.
Come here for antiques and curios,
shoes, a photography store and the
very hip Loft Market on the top floor.

Smock

31 Drury Street, Temple Bar (613
9000/www.smock .ie). All cross-city
buses/Luas St Stephen's Green.
Open 10.30am-6pm Mon-Sat.
Map p57 D3 ❺

Having relocated in mid 2008 to this
ultra chic site (a lovingly restored
townhouse that looks like it has been
imported from SoHo), Smock is still one
of the hippest women's boutiques on
this or any other block. Vintage jewellery and accessories are also sold.

Nightlife

Andrews Lane

NEW *9-17 Andrews Lane (478 0766).*
Map p57 D2 ❺

Andrews Lane used to be a theatre
until July 2008, when it reopened under

Chic and cheerful

How to cut a dash without splashing the cash.

Powerscourt Townhouse Centre

In this time of economic uncertainty, so-called 'frugalistas' are shying away from the usual pan-European labels and looking for new ways to revive their wardrobes. Fortunately, some of Dublin's best-kept secrets are proving that battling the credit crunch doesn't have to mean compromising on style.

The **Loft Market**, inside the Powerscourt Townhouse Centre (p68), is Dublin's first New York-style indoor market, a place where local and international designers can display their fashion and art every weekend. With a live DJ on Saturday afternoons, it dishes up an eclectic mix of everything from customised ballerina pumps to sparkling couture pieces sourced from Barcelona and Paris.

The busy **Café Market** is held on Curved Street on the last Saturday afternoon of every month, inside movie resource centre Filmbase (www.filmbase.ie). Freshly baked cakes and home-made lemonade are served up between stalls that mix new and vintage designs along with art, photography and jewellery.

Far more peaceful is **Cow's Lane Fashion and Design Market**, which takes place just around the corner every Saturday from 10.30am to 5pm. Here you'll find one-offs from Irish labels such as belleElik, which champions ethical style through everything from fair trade silk scarves to recycled cashmere.

Environmental awareness has also led to the swap-o-rama. The idea is simple: bring along your unwanted clothing, pile it into one collective heap and proceed on a rummage that ends with jeans being turned into handbags and oversized T-shirts into halter necks. Such swap soirées are often organised by word of mouth, and so can be difficult for visitors to latch on to. If you're lucky enough to find one, you may come away with some of the most inventive tailoring you'll find anywhere. Nothing says 'recession chic' like a dress expertly made from a Bob the Builder sleeping bag.

Fallon & Byrne p68

new ownership as a nightclub. Since then it has taken the city by storm, with amazing club nights, unannounced big-name DJs and all kinds of spin-off events.

Button Factory

Curved Street (670 9202/ww2. buttonfactory.ie). All cross-city buses. **Map** p57 D2 🟢
The Button Factory – refurbished version of the Temple Bar Music Centre, where sound quality and atmosphere mattered less than beer and decibels – opened in 2007. With a new layout and sound system, it's a useful addition to the Dublin music scene.

Eamonn Doran's

3A Crown Alley (679 9114). All cross-city buses. **Open** noon-2.30am Mon-Sat; noon-1am Sunday. **Map** p57 D2 🟢
Eamonn Doran's replaced the Rock Garden when its star dimmed in the late '90s; the new owner kept the metallic decor in the basement and refurbished the upstairs bar. Doran's is slowly gaining prominence as a launch pad for Irish rock acts like the Things and Halite.

George

89 South Great George's Street (478 2983/www.capitalbars.com). All cross-city buses. **Open** 12.30-11.30pm Mon, Tue; 12.30pm-2.30am Wed-Sat; 2.30pm-1am Sun. **Map** p57 D3 🟢
The hub of gay life in Dublin since the early 1990s, the George has expanded to become two bars and a club that's a hotbed most nights – especially on Sundays, when the Shirley Temple-Bar hosts a notorious bingo session.

JJ Smyth's

12 Aungier Street (475 2565/www. jjsmyths.com). Bus 16, 16A, 19, 19A, 83/Luas St Stephen's Green. **Open** 10.30am-11.30pm Mon-Thur; 10.30am-12.30am Fri, Sat; 12.30-11pm Sun. No credit cards. **Map** p57 D4 🟢
One of the city's oldest jazz and blues venues, Smyth's does good music every night but Wednesdays. There's an acoustic jam session on the first

Tuesday of every month, and fine jazz on Monday, Thursday and Sunday. Downstairs is a regular, old-fashioned Dublin boozer – and very nice with it.

Olympia

72 Dame Street (679 3323/tickets 0818 719 330/www.mcd.ie/venues). All cross-city buses/Luas Jervis. **Map** p56 C2 🟢
The Olympia is one of Dublin's old music halls, a fabulous place with red velvet seats and boxes. The acoustics are excellent, and it has hosted the likes of Radiohead, Bowie and Blur.

Purty Kitchen

34/35 Essex Street East (677 0945/ www.purtykitchen.com). All cross-city buses. **Open** noon-2.30am Mon-Sat; noon-11pm Sun.. **Map** p56 C2 🟢
This swish three-floor bar and club on Essex Street extended its reach further with the launch of a striking new rooftop terrace bar in the autumn of 2008. The smart bar has dark wood aplenty, and the entertainment spaces host live music six nights a week. Gay cabaret takes to the stage on Sundays at 9pm.

Think Tank

NEW *24-25 Eustace Street (635 9991) All cross-city buses/Luas Jervis.* **Open** *Live music* from 8pm. *Music club* 11pm-2.30am daily. Map p57 D2 🟢
A small-scale rock venue in the city centre, this basement bar has a small stage that puts musicians and audience pretty much face to face. Acts tend to be local rock bands on the way up, with a few low-key international names.

Arts & leisure

Gaiety

King Street South (677 1717/www. gaietytheatre.ie). All cross-city buses/ Luas St Stephen's Green **Map** p57 D4 🟢
The Gaiety is a lovely Victorian chocolate box-style theatre that hosts the Christmas pantos and the spring opera season. It also does classic Irish plays and West End shows during the Dublin Theatre Festival (p34).

Gallery Number One

NEW *1 Castle Street (478 9090/www. gallerynumberone.com). All cross-city buses/Luas Jervis.* **Open** 11am-6pm Mon-Wed, Fri, Sat; 11am-8pm Thur; 1-6pm Sun. **Map** p56 C3 ⓺⓸

Gallery Number One exhibits an interesting selection of contemporary works: it aims to 'celebrate the link between art, music and popular culture', which might mean anything from displaying photographs taken by Pattie Boyd to a major show of paintings by Ronnie Wood.

Gallery of Photography

Meeting House Square (671 4654/www.irish-photography.com). All cross-city buses/Luas Jervis. **Open** 11am-6pm Tue-Sat; 1-5pm Sun. **Map** p57 D2 ⓺⓹

This gallery's permanent collection of 20th-century Irish art is run in conjunction with monthly exhibitions by Irish and international photographers.

Gorry Gallery

20 Molesworth Street (679 5319/www. gorrygallery.ie). All cross-city buses/ Luas St Stephen's Green. **Open** 11.30am-5.30pm Mon-Fri; 11am-2pm Sat (during exhibitions). No credit cards. **Map** p57 F3 ⓺⓺

This gallery is a lovely space, where an old-world atmosphere is combined with some wonderfully eccentric touches. The Gorry sells Irish art from the 18th to the 21st centuries.

Graphic Studio Gallery

Through the Arch, off Cope Street (679 8021/www.graphicstudiodublin.com). All cross-city buses/Luas Jervis. **Open** 10am-5.30pm Mon-Fri; 11am-5pm Sat. **Map** p57 D2 ⓺⓻

A Temple Bar gem. Works on paper by Irish and international contemporary printmakers are displayed on two atmospheric levels; affordable works in folders start at €90.

Irish Film Institute

6 Eustace Street (679 5744/www.irish film.ie). All cross-city buses/Luas Jervis. **Map** p57 D2 ⓺⓼

The IFI occupies a wonderfully converted 17th-century building; it has two screens, a bookshop, a public film archive and a busy bar that serves decent food and is popular in its own right. Come here for serious, non-commercial film: indie, foreign, experimental, documentary and classic. It also runs educational screenings and the annual Reel Ireland festival, which shows the latest work by the country's up-and-coming film-makers.

Irish Modern Dance Theatre

Rear 44, Essex Street East (671 5113/ www.irishmoderndancetheatre.com). **Map** p56 C2 ⓺⓽

Performing ambitious new works to original music by young composers, IMDT, run by progressive Dublin-born choreographer John Scott, collaborates frequently with artists such as the dance filmmaker Charles Atlas, and it has strong links with international dance companies.

Project Arts Centre

39 Essex Street East (box office 881 9613/www.project.ie). All cross-city buses/Luas Jervis. **Map** p56 C2 ⓻⓪

PAC began 40 years ago as a visual arts project in the foyer of the Gate (p101), before settling into these refurbished premises in 2000. Its three multifunctional spaces host theatre, dance, video and film, music, debates and performance pieces, making this Dublin's main venue for the cutting edge.

Temple Bar Gallery & Studios

5-9 Temple Bar (671 0073/www. templebargallery. com). All cross-city buses. **Open** 11am-6pm Tue, Wed, Fri, Sat; 11am-7pm Thur. **Map** p57 D2 ⓻⓵

Essentially a non-profit organisation, these are the most coveted artists' studios in Dublin. At the end of each year they organise a fundraising show in which much of the work produced by its resident artists is sold. You can schedule a studio visit and meet the artists, 30 of whom work upstairs. Displays here are invariably challenging and uninhibited.

St Stephen's Green

St Stephen's Green & Around

As is clear from the rows of stern grey Georgian townhouses that line up around its lush squares, the area around St Stephen's Green was once a well-to-do residential neighbourhood. These days, however, it's the city's commercial hub, where most of Dublin's major offices are to be found – as well as the highly regarded **National Gallery of Ireland** and a clutch of museums headed up by the **National Museum of Archaeology & History**.

It's a beautiful neighbourhood in which to lose yourself on a long, meandering walk – not only around the Green itself, but among some of the lesser-known parks and gardens, and along the historic streets that lead down to the quiet waters of the Grand Canal. Many visitors see little beyond Merrion Square (where it seems every famous 19th-century Dubliner lived at one time or another), but why not stretch your legs a little further and take a walk along the canal – and onwards to the Liffey?

Sights & museums

Jewish Museum
3 Walworth Road, Portobello (490 1857). Bus 16, 16A, 19, 19A, 22, 22A/Luas Harcourt. **Open** *May-Sept* 11am-3.30pm Tue, Thur, Sun. *Oct-Apr* 10.30am-2.30pm Sun. **Admission** free. **Map** p74 A5 ❶
This collection of documents and artefacts relating to the Jewish community

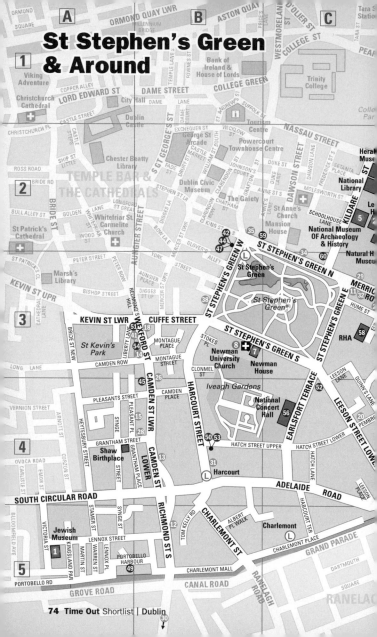

St Stephen's Green & Around

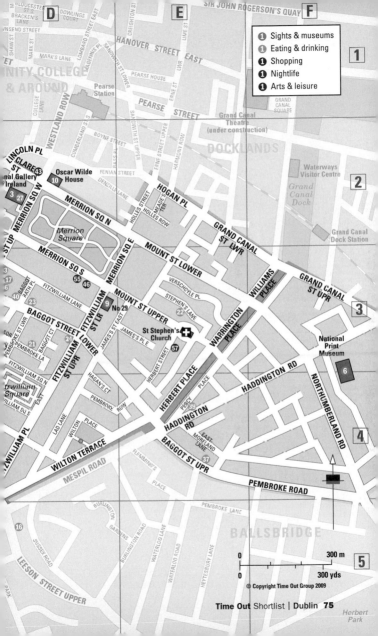

Legend

- ① Sights & museums
- ① Eating & drinking
- ① Shopping
- ① Nightlife
- ① Arts & leisure

TRINITY COLLEGE & AROUND

SIR JOHN ROGERSON'S QUAY

HANOVER STREET EAST

Pearse Station

PEARSE STREET

Grand Canal Theatre (under construction)

DOCKLANDS

Grand Canal Square

Waterways Visitor Centre

Grand Canal Dock

Grand Canal Dock Station

LINCOLN PL
LINCLARE ST
43
nal Gallery Ireland
21

Oscar Wilde House
10

MERRION SQ N

HOGAN PL

GRAND CANAL ST LWR

GRAND CANAL ST UPR

Merrion Square

MERRION SQ E

MOUNT ST LOWER

WILLIAMS PLACE

MERRION SQ S
55
46

Baggot Rath Pl
FITZWILLIAM LANE
17
6
40
23

MOUNT ST UPPER
9 No 29

VERSCHOYLE PL

STEPHEN'S LANE
22

WARRINGTON PLACE

National Print Museum
6

BAGGOT STREET LOWER
21
21

FITZWILLIAM ST LR

St Stephen's Church
57

HADDINGTON RD

NORTHUMBERLAND RD

FITZWILLIAM ST UPR

Fitzwilliam Square

HERBERT PLACE

PERCY PLACE

WILLIAM SQ S

WILTON PLACE

HAGAN'S CT

PEMBROKE ROW

HADDINGTON RD

EAST MORELAND LANE

WILTON TERRACE

LAD LANE

MESPIL ROAD

BAGGOT ST UPR
37

PEMBROKE ROAD

BALLSBRIDGE

BURLINGTON GARDENS

PEMBROKE LANE

16

SUSSEX ROAD

LEESON STREET UPPER

WATERLOO LANE

HETTESBURY LANE

0   300 m
0   300 yds

© Copyright Time Out Group 2009

Herbert Park

Jewish Museum p73

of Ireland includes a reconstruction of a late 19th-century kitchen typical of a Jewish home and, upstairs, a synagogue with ritual fittings. The exhibition covers events like the 1920s pogroms against the Jews of Limerick.

Leinster House

Kildare Street (618 3000/www. oireachtas.ie). All cross-city buses/Luas St Stephen's Green. **Open** *Tours* (when Parliament is not in session) 10.30am, 11.30am, 2.30pm, 3.30pm Mon-Fri. **Admission** free. **Map** p74 C2 ❷

Leinster House is the seat of the Irish Parliament, made up of the Dáil (lower house) and the Seanad (senate or upper house). It was built by Richard Castle between 1745 and 1748 for the Earl of Kildare, who became Duke of Leinster in 1766. The Seanad meets in the sumptuous North Wing Saloon; the Dáil in a rather prosaic room added as a lecture theatre in 1897. The house has two formal fronts – one on Kildare Street, designed to look like a townhouse, and one on Merrion Square – that are connected by a long central corridor.

National Gallery of Ireland

Merrion Square West (661 5133/www. nationalgallery.ie). All cross-city buses/ Luas St Stephen's Green. **Open** 9.30am-5.30pm Mon-Wed, Fri, Sat; 9.30am-8.30pm Thur; noon-5.30pm Sun. **Admission** free. **Map** p75 D2 ❸

This gallery houses a small but fine collection of European works from the 14th to the 20th centuries, including paintings by Caravaggio, Tintoretto, Titian, Monet, Degas, Goya, Vermeer and Picasso. A room is devoted to painter Jack Yeats, who developed an impressionistic style particularly suited to the Irish landscape. The smaller British collection is also impressive, with works by Hogarth, Landseer and Gainsborough; every January an exhibition of Turner's watercolours draws art lovers from all over the world. Giovanni Lanfranco's magnificent *Last Supper* (in the equally impressive Baroque Room) is worth seeing. The gallery's fabulous Millennium Wing has been a big draw since it opened.

National Library of Ireland

Kildare Street (603 0200/www.nli.ie). All cross-city buses/Luas St Stephen's Green. **Open** 9.30am-9pm Mon-Wed; 9.30am-5pm Thur, Fri; 9.30am-1pm Sat. **Admission** free. **Map** p74 C2 ❹

The National Library is a research facility, but some parts of it are open to the public: the grand domed Reading Room – where Stephen Dedalus gives his views on Shakespeare in *Ulysses* – and the Exhibition Room, which plays host to changing displays from the Library's extensive collections. A multimillion euro extension to increase exhibition, reading and repository space has been given the green light.

National Museum of Archaeology & History

Kildare Street (677 7444/www. museum.ie). All cross-city buses/Luas St Stephen's Green. **Open** 10am-5pm Tue-Sat; 2-5pm Sun. **Admission** free. Tours €2. **Map** p74 C2 ❺

The National Museum is deservedly one of Dublin's most popular attractions. The 19th-century building is squeezed in beside Leinster House; its domed entrance hall, or Rotunda, looks like a Victorian take on the Pantheon, with windows on the upper gallery that appear to cave inwards. The most striking exhibition among its many excellent pieces is Ór, a collection of Bronze Age Irish gold displayed in vast glass cases on the ground floor. Further along are examples of extraordinarily intricate sacred and secular metalwork dating from the Iron Age to the Middle Ages, as well as displays of well-preserved artefacts from prehistoric and Viking Ireland.

National Print Museum

Garrison Chapel, Beggars Bush, Haddington Road (660 3770/www. iol.ie/~npmuseum). Bus 5, 7, 7A, 45, 63/DART Grand Canal Dock. **Open** 9am-5pm Mon-Fri; 2-5pm Sat, Sun. **Admission** €3.50; €2 reductions; €7 family. No credit cards. **Map** p75 F3 ❻

This display of printing equipment is not boring – which is a feat in itself. In fact, it's truly interesting. The Beggars

Bush building was once a barracks, and the central garrison houses the Irish Labour History Museum, filled with documents relating to labour and industrial history. The guided tours are entertaining and informative.

Newman House

85-86 St Stephen's Green South (716 7422). All cross-city buses/Luas St Stephen's Green. **Open** (tours only) June-Aug 2pm, 3pm, 4pm Tue-Fri. **Admission** €5; €4 reductions. No credit cards. **Map** p74 B3 ❼

These conjoined townhouses are probably Dublin's finest 18th-century Georgian buildings that are open to the public. Built in 1738 for Irish MP Hugh Montgomery, no.85 has a sombre façade that hides a spacious, elegant interior; the famous Apollo Room has lavish panels depicting Apollo and the Muses, and a magnificent saloon has allegories promoting prudent economy and government. No.86 was begun in 1765 by Richard Whaley, father of notorious gambler Buck. Head to the top of the house via the back stairs to see poet Gerard Manley Hopkins's spartan bedroom and study.

Newman University Church

87A St Stephen's Green South (478 0616/www.universitychurch.ie). All cross-city buses/Luas St Stephens Green. **Open** 9am-5pm Mon-Fri; 9am-5.30pm Sat; 9.30am-4pm Sun. **Admission** free. **Map** p74 B3 ❽

At one time, this church was UCD's answer to Trinity College. Now it's a favourite setting for society weddings, although its opulent, neo-Byzantine interior found little favour when it was completed in 1856. One of Dublin's most fashionable churches.

Number Twenty-Nine

29 Fitzwilliam Street Lower (702 6165/www.esb.ie/numbertwentynine). Bus 6, 7, 10, 45/DART Grand Canal Dock. **Open** 10am-5pm Tue-Sat; noon-5pm Sun. **Admission** *Guided tours* €6; €3 reductions; free under-16s. **Map** p75 D3 ❾

This restored 18th-century merchant house is presented as a middle-class dwelling circa 1790-1820. From furniture – comfortable rather than opulent – and paintings to toys and personal effects, the interior of this property is a treasure trove of Georgian style. History buffs will also be intrigued by the collection of prints, oil paintings and watercolours, many of which show interesting views of the city.

Oscar Wilde House

American College Dublin, 1 Merrion Square (662 0281/www.amcd.ie). All cross-city buses. **Open** *Guided tours* by appointment only (min 25 people). **Admission** €8. No credit cards. **Map** p75 D2 ❿

Wilde's house is only open to large groups – though a big refurb has left it looking good, so if you do manage to get inside, you won't be disappointed. He lived here until 1878; the restored interior includes the surgery and Lady Speranza's drawing room.

Eating & drinking

Bang Café

11 Merrion Row (676 0898/www.bang restaurant. com). All cross-city buses/ Luas St Stephen's Green. **Open** 12.30-3pm, 6-10.30pm Mon-Wed; 12.30-3pm, 6-11pm Thur-Sat. **€€€. Modern Irish. Map** p74 C3 ⓫

This hip venue has a chef from London's Ivy restaurant, cool, minimalist interiors with brash art, and a menu full of dishes you want to eat. The scallops with mousseline potatoes and pancetta is an Ivy classic, and pan-fried fillet of Irish beef with sautéed girolles, braised shallots and dauphinoise potatoes is the stuff of comforting dreams. Cocktails are good, and the customers rather fabulous. Quite possibly the most fashionable restaurant in the city.

Bernard Shaw Bar

11-12 South Richmond Street, (085 712 8342). Bus 19, 122, 16, 16A/ Luas Harcourt. **Open** 4pm-11.30pm Sun-Thur; 4pm-12.30am Fri, Sat. **Bar. Map** p74 B5 ⓬

A proper, 113-year-old Irish boozer, under new management since 2006. The Bernard Shaw has kept its frayed-at-the-edges charm, but the new owners have added extra fun: DJs appear nightly, playing everything from rock to hip hop and reggae to dubstep. The bar is also a gallery space, and hosts quirky events such as record fairs and film clubs.

Bleeding Horse

24 Camden Street Upper (475 2705). Bus 16, 16A, 19, 19A, 49N, 83/ Luas Harcourt. **Open** noon-12.30am Mon-Wed; noon-1am Thur; noon-2am Fri, Sat; noon-11.30pm Sun. **Bar**. **Map** p74 B4 ⑬

The Bleeding Horse on Camden Street Upper has been here for two centuries, and attracts a pleasant crowd of locals and an energetic student group. The bar sprawls over several levels: the connecting rooms downstairs have heavy beams and a medieval atmosphere, and there's a fairly good restaurant upstairs. The place can get busy at weekends.

Bóbó's

ᴺᴱᵂ *22 Wexford Street (400 5750/ www.bobos.ie). All cross-city buses/Luas St Stephen's Green.* **Open** 11am-11pm daily. **€**. **American**. Map p74 B3 ⑭

Taking the diner look and giving it a nifty After Noah spin, this excellent joint serves up peerless patties, 'proper chubby chips' and delicious malts, shakes and juices. Try the delicious Chimicurri, a fiery blend of chimicurri sauce and chorizo on a fat, juicy burger.

Cake Café

ᴺᴱᵂ *Daintree Stationers, Pleasants Place (478 9394 www.thecakecafe.ie). Bus 14, 14A, 15, 15A, 15B, 16A, 65/Luas Harcourt.* **Open** 8am-8pm Mon-Fri; 10am-6pm Sat. **Café**. **Map** p74 B4 ⑮

This adorable new venture already has a loyal following. Inside, it looks a bit like a 1950s kitchen, but the terrace is funkier, with murals and an overhanging scaffold of bamboo poles. The food consists of the eponymous cakes (all home-made, all delicious), biscuits, pies and cupcakes, sandwiches, great

Newman House

ST PATRICK'S HOUSE OF THE CATHOLIC UNIVERSITY UNIVERSITY COLLEGE 1854-19

JOHN HENRY NEWMAN RECTOR 1852-59

GERARD MANLEY HOPKINS PROFESSOR OF GREEK 1884-

JAMES AUGUSTINE JOYCE STUDENT 1899-1902

DUBLIN BY AREA

Number Twenty-Nine p78

DUBLIN BY AREA

salads (caramelised pear, blue cheese and walnut, say) and some more ambitious hot dishes. A treasure.

Canal Bank Café

146 Upper Leeson Street (664 2135/ www.canalbankcafe.com). All cross-city buses/Luas Charlemont. **Open** 10am-11pm Mon-Fri; 11am-11pm Sat, Sun. **Café**. Map p75 D5 ⑯

This smart and easygoing café has young, sassy staff and an American-influenced menu of omelettes, soups, burgers, steak sandwiches and quesadillas, as well as more grown-up dishes like sole on the bone or moules frites. Brunch is pleasant too. Be sure to ask for a window table.

Cellar

Merrion Hotel, 22 Merrion Street Upper (603 0630 www.merrionhotel. com). All cross-city buses/Luas St Stephen's Green. **Open** 7-10.30am, 12.30-2pm, 6-10pm Mon-Fri; 7-11am, 6-10pm Sat; 7-11am, 12.30-2.30pm, 6-10pm Sun. €€€. **Modern Irish**. Map p75 D3 ⑰

Dramatic vaulted ceiling, a quiet vibe and excellent wines: this is an immaculate operation serving casual and contemporary classics (steamed smoked salmon with asparagus, poached egg and lemon oil, for instance). It also has a gorgeous terrace for al fresco dining in the warmer months.

Corner Stone

40 Wexford Street (478 9816). Bus 55, 61, 62, 83/Luas St Stephen's Green. **Open** 11am-11.30pm Mon-Thur; 11am-2.30am Fri; 4pm-2am Sat. **Bar**. Map p74 B3 ⑱

The façade on this corner building has been restored in recent years, and is a pleasing introduction to the (also remodelled) bar inside. The decor is contemporary but not overly hip, with subdued lighting and leather seats in cool shades. Lunches are tasty, and the upstairs lounge hosts live music and late drinking at weekends.

Da Vincenzo

133 Leeson Street Upper (660 9906). All cross-city buses/Luas Charlemont. **Open** noon-11pm Mon-Fri; 1-11pm Sat; 1-10pm Sun. €€€. **Italian**. Map p75 D5 ⑲

This cosy old-timer is always busy. Try to book the snug table on the left as you walk in (no.21) – it's one of the nicest spots in town. Skip the average pastas and order the well-made pizza, keeping the topping simple: a simple margherita with some mushrooms and garlic is one of the best options.

DAX

23 Upper Pembroke Street (676 1494/ www.dax.ie). All cross-city buses/Luas St Stephen's Green. **Open** 12.30-2pm, 6.30-11pm Tue-Fri; 6-11pm Sat. €€€. **French**. Map p74 C4 ⑳

See box p83.

Diep Le Shaker

55 Pembroke Lane (661 1829/www. diep.net). All cross-city buses/Luas St Stephen's Green. **Open** noon-2.30pm, 5-11pm Mon-Thur; noon-11pm Fri; 6-11pm Sat. €€. **Thai**. Map p75 D3 ㉑

Big, bright and busy, this tasty Thai has plenty of great stuff on the menu: things like red prawn curry or stir-fried chicken with cashew nuts and dried chilli. The Diep brand (there's also a noodle bar and a couple of home delivery outposts) has come to be associated with comforting, delicious Thai classics, and it rarely disappoints.

Dobbins

15 Stephen's Lane (661 3321/www. dobbins.ie). All cross-city buses/Luas St Stephen's Green. **Open** 12.30-2.30pm, 6-9.30pm Mon-Fri; 6-10pm Sat; noon-3pm Sun. €€€. **Irish**. Map p75 E3 ㉒

Full of politicos and men in suits, this is one of the best places for a long, boozy lunch. The wine list is endless, and the food is all very meat and potatoes (rack of lamb, crispy duck, suckling pig). The waiters seem to have been here forever, the location is discreet, and fun is guaranteed.

Doheny & Nesbitt

5 Baggot Street Lower (676 2945). Bus 10, 11, 11A Luas St Stephen's Green. **Open** 10.30am-12.30am Mon-Thur; 10.30am-12.30am Fri, Sat; 12.30-11pm Sun. **Pub**. Map p75 D3 ㉓

At weekends, this glorious old pub on Baggot Street Lower is packed with lawyers getting squiffy and quoting Blackstone at each other. It's quieter during the week, when you can gaze at your reflection in the polished wood

and enjoy a pleasant, contemplative drink. In summer and on rugby days, it's mayhem again.

L'Ecrivain

109A Baggot Street Lower (661 1919 www.lecrivain.com). All cross-city buses/ Luas St Stephen's Green. **Open** 12.30-2pm, 7-10pm Mon-Fri; 7-11pm Sat. €€€€. **Haute cuisine**. Map p75 D3 ㉔

Where traditional Irish gets a gourmet twist: the oysters in Guinness sabayon are famous. Suits abound at lunch, but in the evening this is the perfect spot for a romantic dinner. And although the cooking is highly accomplished – spring lamb, perhaps, served in the form of a moussaka with green peas, mint, feta and confit aubergine – the place is also refreshingly informal.

Ely

22 Ely Place (676 8986/www.elywine bar.ie). All cross-city buses/Luas St Stephen's Green. **Open** noon-11.30pm Mon-Thur; noon-12.30am Fri; 1pm-12.30am Sat. €€€. **Wine bar/Irish**. Map p75 C3 ㉕

Cosy and smart, with brick walls and big armchairs, Ely has a vast wine list that is possibly the best in the country. The organic beef burger or Irish classics like Kilkea oysters, bangers and mash and an Irish cheese plate, is the perfect partner to the wine. Conspicuously affluent, but still good fun.

Flannery's

6 Camden Street Lower (478 2238). All cross-city buses/Luas Harcourt. **Open** noon-2.30am Mon-Fri; 1pm-2.30am Sat, Sun. **Bar**. Map p74 B4 ㉖

Unashamed of its less-than-appealing exterior, Flannery's is at its busiest at the weekend, when a crowd of nurses, teachers and Gardaí pack out the bar. Ideal for a night out with single friends.

Gallery Café

National Gallery of Ireland, Merrion Square West (663 3500). All cross-city buses/Luas St Stephen's Green. **Open** 9.30am-5pm Mon-Wed, Fri, Sat; 9.30am-8pm Thur; noon-5pm Sun. **Café**. Map p75 D2 ㉗

The National Gallery's Millennium Wing houses this bright, white, funkily furnished café, whose arty tourists give it a pleasingly international vibe. There's nothing too filling here, just coffee, tea, scones and snacks.

Havana

3 Camden Market, Grantham Place (476 0046 www.havana.ie). Bus 16, 19, 122/Luas Harcourt. **Open** 11am-10.30pm Mon-Wed; 11am-11.30pm Thur; Fri; 1-11.30pm Sat. **€**. **Tapas**. **Map** p74 B4 ㉓

A small tapas bar that's always ready for fun, Havana has pretty decor, staff and customers. Food can be disappointing, but it's cheap, the music is hopping, and some customers tell of tables being moved aside for dancing.

Hugo's

🆕 *6 Merrion Row (676 5955). All cross-city buses/Luas St Stephen's Green.* **Open** noon- 11pm Mon- Fri; 11am-11pm Sat, Sun. **€€€**. **Modern Irish**. **Map** p74 C3 ㉙ See box p83.

Jo'Burger

🆕 *137 Rathmines Road Lower (491 3731 www.joburger.ie). All cross-city buses/Luas Charlemont/Harcourt.* **Open** noon-11pm Mon- Thur; noon-midnight Fri, Sat; noon-10pm Sun. **€**. **American**. **Map** p74 B5 ㉚

Jo'Burger pulls off the clever trick of looking cool but still serving up a tasty, lively and affordable night out. Long communal tables are surrounded by pop art murals and chintzy wallpaper, and the all-burgers menu lists straight-up versions or ones with cheeses, relishes, mango salsa and more. A hit.

Odeon

57 Harcourt Street (478 2088/ www.odeon.ie). Bus 14, 15, 16/ Luas Harcourt. **Open** noon-11.30pm Mon-Wed; noon-12.30am Thur; noon-2.30am Fri, Sat; noon-11pm Sun. **Bar**. **Map** p74 B4 ㉛

The Odeon's impressive façade tells you what to expect once inside. There aren't too many seats, but nobody really cares: people come here to see and be seen on a sea of polished floorboards under vaulted ceilings. It's not cheap: you pay for the atmosphere and the style. It's especially pleasant on a Sunday, when you can fritter the afternoon away with free newspapers or watch a classic film on the big screen.

O'Donoghue's

15 Merrion Row (660 7194/lounge 676 2807/www.odonoghuesbar.com). All cross-city buses/Luas St Stephen's Green. **Open** 10.30am-11.30pm Mon-Thur; 10.30am-12.30am Fri, Sat; 12.30-11pm Sun. **Pub**. **Map** p74 C3 ㉜

Impromptu jam sessions are a staple here, and outfits like the Dubliners play regularly. The crowd is a mix of genuine locals and visitors, young and old. The pub can be a little claustrophobic (especially mid session), but there's an excellent back alley smoking area.

Pearl

20 Merrion Street Upper (661 3627/ www.pearl-brasserie.com). All cross-city buses/Luas St Stephen's Green. **Open** noon-2.30pm, 6-10.30pm Mon-Fri; 6-10.30pm Sat, Sun. **€€€**. **French**. **Map** p75 D3 ㉝

Great attention to detail has gone into this elegant little place, with its pretty furniture, modern art and funky fish tanks. The bar area serves oysters, champagne and (during the day) delicious soup, croque monsieurs and steak sandwiches. Dinner is fancier: monkfish with ginger confit, or seared scallops with coriander seeds, tomato sauce and chervil. The long wine list is affordable and dangerously tempting.

Peploe's

St Stephen's Green (676 3144/www. peploes.com). All cross-city buses/ Luas St Stephen's Green. **Open** noon-10.30pm Mon-Sat. **€€€**. **Wine bar**. **Map** p74 C3 ㉞ See box p83.

Il Posto

10 St Stephen's Green (679 4769/www.ilpostorestaurant.com). All cross-city buses/Luas St Stephen's Green. **Open** noon-2pm, 5.30-10pm Mon-Wed; noon-2pm, 5.30-10.30pm

Green bottles...

This part of the city is paradise for winelovers.

Hugo's

Some of Dublin's top wine bars are located on the Green, which means there are somewhere near 500 bottles of truly excellent vino within a short walk of each other.

The newest and very welcome addition to the line-up is **Hugo's** (p82). With its smart aquamarine frontage and chic interior of gold patterned wallpaper and brick walls, Hugo's has a wine list that's expansive but not expensive, with a good showing of bottles from around the world. The food is no afterthought either: dishes like plum stuffed pork tenderloin, seared scallops with wilted greens and curry butter, and chicory, rocquefort and candied pecan salad are beautifully done.

Another bar that matches good wines with good food is the plush, subterranean **DAX** (p81) – which, like many other basement addresses, has to work a lot harder than its street-level counterparts: after all, it needs to entice customers with something more than an inviting scene in a window. Food here is either French 'tapas' by the bar, or excellent, formal fare in the dining room.

Last but not least, there's **Peploe's** (p82), considered by many to be the best wine bar in town. It's a truly sophisticated joint, its rooms decked out with wood, murals and crisp table linen, patrolled by smartly kitted-out staff, and filled with the low hum of intelligent conversation and quietly swinging jazz. It's fast becoming a top address for a fun Friday lunch – full of local heroes and business gurus – and has long been popular as a retreat for the city's cultured set to have their casual evening meals. Chef Sebastian Scheer turns out dishes like crêpe risotto with wilted rocket or loin of free-range pork with a pine nut and apricot gratin. The wine list is obviously very good and very long, and is well worth checking out, even if it's just for a glass of wine at the bar.

DUBLIN BY AREA

Thur, Fri; noon-2.30pm, 5.30-10.30pm Sat; 5.30-10pm Sun. €€€. **Italian**. **Map** p74 B2 ⑤

This cosy, warm basement restaurant serves decent Italian grub. Lunch can be disappointing atmosphere-wise, except on a busy Friday, but dinner makes up for it. Grilled swordfish with lemon and olive oil, and good old chicken supreme wrapped in pancetta are very tasty. Portions are huge, the side orders are good (not an after-thought), and the place is usually hopping.

Restaurant Patrick Guilbaud

The Merrion Hotel, 22 Merrion Street Upper (676 4192/www.restaurant patrickguilbaud.ie). All cross-city buses/Luas St Stephen's Green. **Open** 12.30-2.15pm, 7.30-10.15pm Tue-Fri; 1-2.15pm, 7.30-10.15pm Sat. €€€€. **Haute cuisine**. **Map** p75 D3 ㊱

Looking every bit as stellar as its two Michelin stars suggest, Guilbaud's is pretty much the top table in town, wheeling out dishes like Wicklow venison fillet in mulled wine, served with apple polenta, crisp muesli, balsamic and grue de cacao reduction. But be warned: if you go off-piste and start ordering cheese, dessert, and a second bottle of wine, you may have to sell your house or spouse to pay the bill.

Searson's

42-44 Baggot Street Upper (660 0330 www.searsons.ie). Bus 10. **Open** 10am-11.30pm Mon-Thur; 12.30pm-1.30am Fri, Sat; 4-11pm Sun. **Pub**. **Map** p75 E4 ㊲

While all around it, pubs bow to the pressure to refurbish and change direction, Searson's sticks to its guns and its rather lovely classic Victorian decor. Punters are professionals, regulars and twentysomethings, and there's an ample smoking area out the back.

Shanahan's

119 St Stephen's Green West (407 0939/www.shanahans.ie). All cross-city buses/Luas St Stephen's Green. **Open** 6-9.45pm Mon-Thur; 12.30-2pm, 6-10.30pm Fri-Sun. €€€€. **Irish**. **Map** p74 B3 ㊳

Some believe this classy steakhouse to be the finest restaurant in the city. Sink your teeth into one of its 12oz filet mignons – perfectly aged, perfectly cut and cooked in state-of-the-art broilers – and you might well be one of them. The setting is slick (chandeliers, gilt mirrors), and the side orders of exquisite creamed spinach and heart-stopping dauphinoise are fab too.

Smyth's

10 Haddington Road (660 6305). Bus 10. **Open** 10am-11.30pm Mon-Thur;

Shanahan's

10.30am-12.30am Fri, Sat; 12.30-11pm Sun. **Pub**. **Map** p75 E4 **39**

Near the Grand Canal, Smyth's is a real neighbourhood pub with a nice, calm atmosphere. An ill-considered renovation a few years back did its best to garble its charms, but it only partially succeeded, and Smyth's remains a quiet, snug and comfortable boozer.

Toner's

139 Baggot Street Lower (676 3090). Bus 10, 11, 11A/Luas St Stephen's Green. **Open** 10.30am-11.30pm Mon-Wed; 10.30am-12.30am Thur-Sat; 12.30-11pm Sun. **Pub**. **Map** p75 D3 **40**

Toner's is an authentic Dublin pub: the character that made it popular still remains, despite some (light) tarting up. At weekends it's packed to the rafters, but gets much quieter in the week. It also holds the honour of being the only pub visited by WB Yeats.

Village

26 Wexford Street (475 8555/www. thevillagevenue.com). Bus 16, 16A, 19, 19A/Luas Harcourt. **Open** 11am-2.30am Mon-Fri; 5pm-2.30am Sun. **Bar**. **Map** p74 B3 **41**

The Village is one of Dublin's newest and best music venues, catering to a wider and more diverse crowd than Whelan's next door (p88). The success of its nightly gigs, however, tends to distract attention from the bar itself, which is attractive and agreeable in its own right. Its striking modern frontage lets in lots of natural light, and this gives way to the cool atmosphere of the main bar. You can eat here at any time of the day, and eat well; Sunday brunch is accompanied by jazz bands.

Shopping

Golden Discs

Stephen's Green Centre (872 4211/ www.goldendiscs.ie). All cross-city buses/Luas St Stephen's Green. **Open** 9am-6pm Mon-Wed, Fri, Sat; 9am-9pm Thur; noon-6pm Sun. **Map** p74 B2 **42**

Handily located right opposite Grafton Street, this Stephen's Green Centre branch of Golden Discs is fast becoming overshadowed by larger international chains, which may be in part because of its dedication to MOR stock.

Henry Jermyn

16 Clare Street (676 0501). All cross-city buses/Luas St Stephen's Green. **Open** 8.30am-6.30pm Mon-Wed, Fri; 8.30am-8pm Thur; 9am-6pm Sat; noon-6pm Sun. **Map** p75 D2 **43**

Keeping the gents of Dublin in hats and threads, this high-end tailor has an exclusive, gentleman's club aesthetic: oil paintings, ornate mantlepieces and other old-world trappings punctuate the racks of pinstripe suits and floor-to-ceiling shelves of double-cuffed shirts. The bespoke suits are as good as you'll find anywhere in town, and there's a tasteful range of ties, cufflinks, umbrellas and felt hats (by Christys' & Company).

Hughes & Hughes

Stephen's Green Centre (478 3060/www. hugheshooks.com). All cross-city buses/ Luas St Stephen's Green. **Open** 9.30am-6pm Mon-Wed, Fri, Sat; 9.30am-8pm Thur; noon-6pm Sun. **Map** p74 B2 **44**

A decent chain with an especially strong selection of Irish fiction, Hughes & Hughes also keeps its eye in with smaller sections on history, cookery and self-help. This branch has a particularly wide-ranging and well-presented stock of junior reading material.

INREDA

71 Lower Camden Street (476 0362/ www.inreda.ie). All cross-city buses/ Luas St Stephen's Green. **Open** 10.30am-6pm Mon-Fri; 11am-6pm Sat. **Map** p74 B4 **45**

Design-literate lighting, furniture, homeware and kitchenware light up this small but stylish shop. Beautiful (and portable) home and kitchen accessories by String, iittala and Stelton will have spontaneous shoppers reaching for the plastic, while more serious, and less wieldy, purchases from the range of Ruben and Moooi furniture and lighting will probably require a little more forward planning.

DUBLIN BY AREA

Louise Kennedy

56 Merrion Square (662 0056/www. louisekennedy.com). All cross-city buses/Luas St Stephen's Green. **Open** 9am-6pm Mon-Sat. **Map** p75 D3
Famed throughout the world for her exquisitely tailored suits and opulent eveningwear, Louise Kennedy is popular with a diverse range of women. Her stunning Georgian salon and home showcase her designs.

Stephen's Green Centre

St Stephen's Green West (478 0888/ www.stephensgreen.com). All cross-city buses/Luas St Stephen's Green. **Open** 9am-7pm Mon-Wed, Fri, Sat; 9am-9pm Thur; 11am-6pm Sun. **Map** p74 B2 ④⑦
This overblown conservatory of a shopping centre makes up in convenience for what it lacks in charm. A wide selection of shops covers three floors and all the bases.

Tyrrell & Brennan

13 Lower Pembroke Street (678 8332/ www.tyrrellbrennan.com). All cross-city
buses/Luas Harcourt. **Open** by appointment. **Map** p75 D3 ④⑧
Affable duo Niall Tyrrell and Donald Brennan have broken the fashion mould with bold designs for real women. Don't expect any fuddy-duddy fashions here: this talented pair does a fine line in ready-to-wear and made-to-order (a hit with Ireland's media types), and some of Ireland's loveliest wedding dresses.

Nightlife

Ballroom of Romance

The Lower Deck, 1 Portobello Harbour (475 1423). Bus 16, 16A, 19, 19A, 122/Luas Charlemont. **Open** times vary. **Map** p74 A5 ④⑨
This monthly alternative live music club, set in an old man's pub, hosts talented new indie acts. You might get the searing post-rock of Terrordactyl one night, and the gentle balladry of Si Schroeder the next. As a starting point for Irish alternative music, Ballroom of Romance is an essential venue.

Henry Jermyn p85

Crawdaddy

NEW *Hatch Street Upper, off Harcourt Street (478 0166/www.crawdaddy.ie). Bus 15A, 15B, 86/Luas Harcourt.* **Open** times vary. **Map** p74 B4 ⑤⓿

Medium-sized Crawdaddy is an exciting new venue that meets the demand for live music with an impressive roster of jazz, world music and rock. It can hold about 300 people, and ticket prices tend to be higher than average; but the place has the atmosphere of a cosy jazz club, and draws acts of the calibre of Courtney Pine and Talvin Singh.

Solas

31 Wexford Street (478 0583/www. solasbars.com). Bus 15, 16, 19, 19A, 55, 61, 62, 83/Luas Harcourt. 11am-2am Fri, Sat; 11am-11.30pm Mon-Thur, Sun. **Map** p74 R3 ⑤①

One of the city's best DJ bars, Solas is a good spot at which to kick off your night. Music starts earlier here than in many other bars, courtesy of a roll call of resident DJs. It's a fun place, but can get absurdly crowded at weekends.

Sugar Club

8 Leeson Street Lower (678 7188/www. thesugarclub.com). Bus 46A/Luas St Stephen's Green. **Open** 8pm-midnight Mon-Thur, 8pm-2.30am Fri-Sun. **Map** p74 C4 ⑤②

One of Dublin's most stylish venues, the Sugar Club has the feel of a hip US jazz bar. The audience gazes down on the musicians from tiered seats with tables; the programme ranges from cabaret and rock to jazz or singer-songwriter sets. Weekday crowds are mainly suits; keep an eye on listings for the likes of KT Tunstall and Crazy P.

Tripod

NEW *Old Harcourt Street Station, Harcourt Street (478 0225/0166/ www.pod.ie). All cross-city buses.* **Open** 7.30pm-2.30am Mon-Sat. **Map** p74 B4 ⑤③

Formerly the famous Red Box, Tripod is one of the city's newest kids on the block. The club doubles as a live venue, but is still renowned for its explosive club nights: on Friday, DJs rustle up a techno/house set; on Saturday, expect more commercial fare. Set in the Pod complex (also home to Crawdaddy; p86), this labyrinthine venue also draws big-name guest DJs like Carl Cox, Erick Morillo and James Lavelle.

Whelan's

25 Wexford Street (478 0766/www. whelanslive.com). Bus 16, 16A, 19, 19A, 122/Luas Harcourt. **Open** noon-2.30am Mon-Sat; noon-1am Sun. *Live music* from 8.30pm Mon-Sat. **Map** p74 B3 **54**

One of the city's best music venues, Whelan's has built an unassailable reputation among Dublin's music fans. It's the stomping ground for most of the city's up-and-coming bands: Damien Rice, David Kitt, the Frames, Paddy Casey and Gemma Hayes all made their first appearances here. The line-up takes in Irish trad, English folk and American roots.

Arts & leisure

Hallward Gallery

65 Merrion Square (662 1482/www. hallwardgallery.com). All cross-city buses/Luas St Stephen's Green. **Open** 11am-5.30pm Tue-Fri; 12.30-4.30pm Sat. **Map** p75 D3 **55**

Despite being tucked into a Georgian basement, this space is surprisingly bright. Works tend to be contemporary Irish art of the tried and tested variety; the quality is always high, with many well-established artists on show – names like John Brennan, Niall Wright, Cormac O'Leary and Maighread Tobin.

National Concert Hall

Earlsfort Terrace (417 0000/ www.nch.ie). All cross-city buses. **Map** p74 C4 **56**

Dublin's main venue for orchestral music was established in 1981, in the Great Hall of what was then University College Dublin. It retains the bland flavour of a lecture theatre, though its acoustics are generally considered excellent. Its annexe, the John Field Room, hosts performances of chamber, jazz, traditional and vocal music.

Peppercanister Gallery

3 Herbert Street (661 1279). Bus 7A, 8, 10. **Open** 10am-5.30pm Mon-Fri; 10am-1pm Sat. **Map** p75 E3 **57**

This gallery is a family-run affair with an informal yet professional vibe. Its artists (mainly Irish) are usually contemporary or early 20th century – names such as Anne Donnelly, Neil Shawcross and Liam Belton.

Royal Hibernian Academy

NEW *15 Ely Place (661 2558/www. royalhibernianacademy.ie). All cross-city buses/Luas St Stephen's Green.* **Open** 11am-7pm Mon-Sat; 2-7pm Sun. **Map** p74 C3 **58**

Utterly transformed after a year of closure, the Royal Hibernian Academy reopened in late 2008 as a smart, sleek new gallery with a suite of artists' studios, café and bookshop. It remains an essentially non-profit organisation, but the RHA's commercial operation continues to hold an annual exhibition (in May) that features more than 1,000 exhibits selected by jury – the best, affordable chance in Dublin to buy the work of highly rated emerging artists.

Rubicon Gallery

10 St Stephen's Green North (670 8055/www.rubicongallery.ie). All cross-city buses/Luas St Stephen's Green. **Open** noon-6pm Tue-Sat. **Map** p74 B2 **59**

Overlooking the treetops of St Stephen's Green, this elegant gallery focuses on international contemporary artists in all media.

Taylor Galleries

16 Kildare Street (676 6055/www. taylorgalleries.ie). All cross-city buses/ Luas St Stephen's Green. **Open** 10am-5.30pm Mon-Fri; 11am-3pm Sat. **Map** p74 C3 **60**

This beautiful gallery fills an entire townhouse. There's a feeling of real elegance to the space, which shows some of Irish modernism's heavyweights – figures such as Louis le Brocquy, William Crozier and Tony O'Malley – alongside artists like Mary Lohan and Timothy Hawkesworth.

General Post Office p90

O'Connell Street & Around

Any Dubliner worth his or her salt will proudly tell you that O'Connell Street is a very wide street – 46 metres (150 feet) – and its buildings are tall (for Dublin). Bookended by sculptures of Ireland's two great constitutional nationalists – Daniel O'Connell and Charles Stewart Parnell – it is, without question, the most imposing thoroughfare in the city, and although it doesn't hold the parliament, it also tends to be the focal point of every political rally. But until recently it was going to seed: it had become a lucrative beat for petty criminals and junkies, its pavements mired in litter, half its fine buildings leased to burger joints, the other half knocked down.

These days, all that has changed. Garda patrol tirelessly, and recent developments include the widening of footpaths, the removal of the old London plane trees, the planting of 200 new trees of various species, the restoration of monuments, the creation of a plaza in front of the **General Post Office** and, of course, the Spire, built in 2003, an enormous stainless steel shard that jabs 120 metres (396 feet) into the sky. All this was done to the usual barrage of criticism (people hated the Spire, loved the old plane trees). But, the street's now looking leafy, prosperous, more pedestrianised, much tidier – in short, much more like the main street of one of Europe's richest countries.

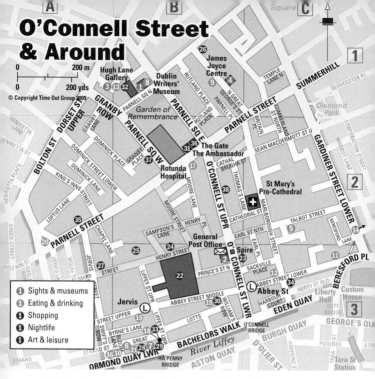

O'Connell Street & Around

Sights & museums

Dublin Writers' Museum

18-19 Parnell Square (872 2077/ www.writersmuseum.com). Bus 3, 10, 11, 13, 16, 19, 22/Luas Abbey Street. **Open** *Sept-May* 10am-5pm Mon-Sat; 11am-5pm Sun. *June-Aug* 10am-6pm Mon-Fri; 10am-5pm Sat; 11am-5pm Sun. **Admission** €7.25; €4.55-€6.10 reductions; €21 family. **Map** p90 B1 ❶

It can be hard to showcase the real achievements of writers, but this small, jam-packed museum does pretty well, featuring unique and well-chosen memorabilia from Swift, Wilde, Yeats, Joyce, Beckett and others. Packed into its rather fusty wooden and glass display cabinets are some unusual and intriguing artefacts, such as the phone from Beckett's Paris apartment, and playbills from the Abbey Theatre's early days. There are also occasional temporary exhibitions.

General Post Office

O'Connell Street (705 7000/www. anpost.ie). All cross-city buses/Luas Abbey Street. **Open** 8am-8pm Mon-Sat. **Admission** free. **Map** p90 B3 ❷

Best known as the site of the Easter Rising in 1916, the GPO remains a potent symbol of Irish independence. Designed by Francis Johnston in 1818, it was almost completely destroyed by fire during the uprising, and had barely been restored six years later when the civil war did further damage to the building. There are still bullet holes in the walls and columns out front, and a series of paintings inside depicts moments from the Easter Rising. At the time of writing, there was talk of a dedicated museum on the 1916 Uprising being installed in the GPO.

Hugh Lane Gallery (Municipal Gallery of Modern Art)

Parnell Square North (222 5550/ www.hughlane.ie). Bus 3, 10, 11, 13, 16, 19, 22/Luas Abbey Street. **Open** 10am-6pm Tue-Thur; 10am-5pm Fri, Sat; 11am-5pm Sun. **Admission** *Gallery* free. *Francis Bacon Studio* €7; €3.50 reductions; free under-18s. Half-price to all 9.30am-12.30pm Tue. **Map** p90 B1 ❸

Celebrating its centenary in 2008, the Municipal Gallery is named after Hugh Lane, nephew of Yeats's friend Lady Gregory and noted art patron who determined to leave his fine collection of French and Irish Impressionist art to the city (provided a suitable gallery was built to house it). Despite a number of vituperative poems from Yeats, Dublin Corporation did not come up with a gallery, forcing Lane to bequeath his pictures to London. At the eleventh hour he stipulated that Dublin could have them if they provided a gallery, but this codicil to his will was unwitnessed when he went down with the other passengers on the Lusitania, torpedoed by a German U-boat in 1915. London stuck to the letter of the law for decades, but the matter was recently settled in Irish favour (though a number of the paintings still rotate between Dublin and London).

James Joyce Centre

35 North Great George's Street (878 8547/www.jamesjoyce.ie). Bus 3, 10, 11, 11A, 13, 16, 16A, 19, 19A, 22/ Luas Abbey Street. **Open** 10am-5pm Tue-Sat. **Admission** €5; €4 reductions. **Walking tours** €10; €8 reductions. **Map** p90 B1 ❹

Joyce never lived here, nor did Leopold Bloom, though a minor character in *Ulysses* – Denis Maginni – held dance classes here. How it came to be the Joyce Centre is that Senator David Norris noticed in the mid 1980s that this beautiful house was decaying, so, deciding to combine his passion for Joyce with his passion for Georgian architecture, he created a trust. The house took 14 years to renovate but, through careful study of old photos, it now looks just as it did in 1904, when Maginni would have been holding his dance classes – the ceiling on the first floor is one of the finest in Dublin.

The top floor has a recreation of Joyce's room in Zurich and a touchscreen history of the publication of *Ulysses*, while the terrace holds the door of 7 Eccles Street (Bloom's house). Highlights from the National Library's recent exhibition on Joyce are also on permanent loan to the Centre, and there are Joycean walking tours every Saturday (at 11am and 2pm).

Eating & drinking

101 Talbot

101 Talbot Street (874 5011/www.101 talbot.com). All cross-city buses/Luas Abbey Street. **Open** 5-11pm Tue-Sat. **€€€**. **International**. **Map** p90 C2 ❺

Casual, but serious about its vegetarian customers, this long-running restaurant nourishes wise locals who pay little attention to food fads. Don't expect any razzmatazz, just straightforward, honest cooking geared to everyone from vegans to carnivores. Dishes include parsnip and sweet potato rösti, West African vegetable and peanut curry, and braised guinea fowl with roasted vegetables and Puy lentils. Chocoholics rave about the chocolate cake, while 101's proximity to theatreland also makes it an ideal spot pre- or post- performances.

Bar Italia

26 Bloom Lane (874 1000/www.bar italia.ie) All cross-city buses/Luas Jervis. **Open** noon-10.30pm Mon-Thur; noon-11pm Fri, Sat; 1-10pm Sun. **€€€**. **Italian**. **Map** p90 B3 ❻

The foodies who own this Italian joint (the team behind the brilliant Dunne &

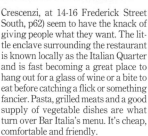

Hugh Lane Gallery p91

Crescenzi, at 14-16 Frederick Street South, p62) seem to have the knack of giving people what they want. The little enclave surrounding the restaurant is known locally as the Italian Quarter and is fast becoming a great place to hang out for a glass of wine or a bite to eat before catching a flick or something fancier. Pasta, grilled meats and a good supply of vegetable dishes are what turn over Bar Italia's menu. It's cheap, comfortable and friendly.

Café Cagliostro

24 Ormond Quay Lower (888 0860). All cross-city buses/Luas Jervis. **Open** 7am-5.30pm Mon-Fri; 8am-5.30pm Sat; 9am-5pm Sun.
Café. Map p90 B3 ⑦
Tiny and fabulous, Café Cagliostro is one of the main tenants in the Bloom Lane courtyard, just off the quays. It features plain, stylish furniture and offers excellent coffee and hot chocolate, as well as a chaste but tasty selection of Italian sandwiches and desserts.

Chapter One

18-19 Parnell Square (873 2266/www. chapteronerestaurant.com). All cross-city buses. **Open** 12.30-2.30pm, 6-11pm Tue-Fri; 6-11pm Sat. €€€€. **Haute cuisine**. Map p90 B1 ⑧
The critics love it, the punters love it, and so will you: a meal at Chapter One is easily the most accessible, affordable and enjoyable fine-dining experience in Dublin. The dining room is warm and tasteful, service is formal but easy-going, and the food is haute cuisine yet down to earth – plus the restaurant is located near to the Gate Theatre (p101), which means that it also offers an excellent pre-theatre set menu. As for the cooking, it is nothing short of spectacular. A starter of sea bream might be served with caponata, pungent olive oil and a basquaise red pepper purée; among the mains, squab pigeon might get a white truffle and honey glaze, while hake and langoustine would be partnered by roast fennel, braised squid and a tomato and

SEAN SCULLY
GALLERY
←

shellfish sauce. All followed, perhaps, by poached meringue with 'amaretto anglaise' and pistachio. Needless to say, the wine list is excellent.

Cobalt Café

16 North Great George's Street (873 0313). All cross-city buses. **Open** 10.30am-4pm Mon-Fri. **Café. Map** p90 B1 ⑨

Housed in a lovingly restored Georgian house, this handsome place is popular with local arty types and office workers. There is no kitchen on site so cakes, sandwiches and soups are bought in. When it is not operating as a café, the Cobalt also hosts drama, music and small-scale performances, which makes it a great place to catch new material. Performances tend to be on the weekends.

Enoteca delle Langhe

24 Lower Ormond Quay (888 0834). All cross-city buses/Luas Jervis. **Open** noon-midnight Mon-Sat. **€€. Italian. Map** p90 B3 ⑩

The cuisine and wines of the Langhe region of Piedmont are at the heart of this excellent operation. If you love beautiful Italian wine, fresh, moreish cooking, and the convivial atmosphere of a group of Italian foodies doing what they love, then you should get down here. The tables and chairs are well spaced, comfortable and look reassuringly expensive. Cheese, tapenade, olives and salamis are served with plenty of bread (great to share, and cheap too). With an Italian deli, coffee shop and two more Italian restaurants in the same development, not for nothing is this area commonly known as the Italian Quarter.

Floridita

[NEW] *Irish Life Mall, Abbey Street Lower (878 1032/www.floriditadublin. com). All cross-city buses/Luas Abbey Street.* **Open** noon-11.30pm Mon-Thur; noon-2.30am Fri; 5pm-2.30am Sat. **Bar. Map** p90 C3 ⑪

From one boozy capital to another, one of Hemingway's favourite Havana bars has opened (under capitalist guise) in Dublin. The former Life Bar has been transformed into the 'seat of the daiquiri' where mixologists serve up mojitos and other Cuban cocktail classics from a lengthy expensive menu that would have made even Hemingway's eyes water.

Flowing Tide

9 Abbey Street Lower (874 4106). All cross-city buses/Luas Abbey Street. **Open** 10.30am-11.30pm Mon-Thur; 10.30am-12.30am Fri, Sat; noon-11pm Sun. **Bar**. **Map** p90 C3 ⑫

A recent renovation has converted the much-loved Tide from a reliable Dublin boozer with a raffish edge into a trendy place with polished wood floors and sleek chrome details. Perhaps the new look is not to all tastes, but the essentials remain the same: the staff and Guinness are as decent as ever, and the bar's location means it still attracts a crowd of actors and audience from the nearby Abbey Theatre.

Hugh Lane Café

Hugh Lane Gallery, Parnell Square North (www.hughlane.ie). All cross-city buses/Luas Abbey Street. **Open** 10am-6pm Tue-Thur; 10am-5pm Fri, Sat; 11am-5pm Sun. **Café**. **Map** p90 B1 ⑬

It may be squirrelled away in the basement of the excellent Hugh Lane Gallery (p91) but this popular café is saved from pokiness by windows looking out on to an enclosed courtyard (complete with water feature) and by its breezy interior of light wood floors and smart white-painted walls. Local office workers and gallery-goers take time out here for coffee, cake, plates of good-quality antipasta, quiches and salads. A compact lunch menu is chalked up on the blackboard.

Isaac Butt Café Bar

Opposite Busáras Station, Store Street (819 7636). All cross-city buses/Luas Busaras. **Open** 5-11.30pm Mon-Wed, Sun; 5pm-2.30am Thur-Sat. **Bar**. **Map** p90 C2 ⑭

A range of techno club nights first made this bar popular among students and backpackers, but the emphasis has recently shifted to live indie music. The warren-like bars provide comfortable refuge from the cares of the world, and there's a big screen for football matches.

Kiely's

37 Upper Abbey Street (872 2100). All cross-city buses/Luas Abbey Street. **Open** 10.30am-11.30pm Mon-Wed, Sun; 10.30am-12.30am Thur; 10.30am-2am Fri, Sat. **Bar**. **Map** p90 B3 ⑮

The Abbey Street entrance leads to a snug, old-style dark wooden bar that's good for quiet pints or watching football in peace. The back of the pub – with the Liffey Street entrance – is 'K3' and couldn't be more different. It's a large, trendy space with a cheery twentysomething crowd. The juxtaposition shouldn't work as well as it does – but one thing both areas have in common is excellent and well-priced food.

Panem

21 Ormond Quay Lower (872 8510). All cross-city buses/Luas Jervis. **Open** 9am-5pm Mon-Sat. No credit cards. **Café**. **Map** p90 B3 ⑯

It may be small but this superb café on Ormond Quay Lower puts a lot of thought and effort into what it does. Hearty granola, moreish muffins and fresh croissants accompany excellent coffee at breakfast, while lunch dishes range from tasty foccacia sarnies and good soups to savoury pasties and a couple of daily pasta dishes. And it's all served up in a fun, stylish space overlooking the river.

Patrick Conway

70 Parnell Street (873 2687). All cross-city buses/Luas Abbey Street. **Open** 10am-11.30pm Mon-Thur; 10am-12.30am Fri, Sat; noon-11pm Sun. No credit cards. **Pub**. **Map** p90 B2 ⑰

A thoughtful pick of interior mood-setters, including candlelight and drapes, gives this Victorian pub a cosy, relaxed atmosphere. Plentiful

The world on a plate

Nowhere epitomises Dublin's multicultural explosion quite like Parnell Street's 'Chinatown'. Although the city's Asian hub is still in its infancy, immigrants have transformed the street into a bustling strip of nearly 20 restaurants offering expats an authentic taste of home.

Chinese restaurants in Dublin used to be drab, characterless institutions where punters paid high prices for run-of-the-mill, westernised Cantonese food. Now, with an estimated 60,000 Chinese people in Ireland, a huge demand for uncompromising Asian cuisine has turned out to be a real boon for local food lovers. An array of traditional dishes from Mongolia to Vietnam can be had for under €10, and despite Asian writing dominating the menus, the injection of much-needed variety and value for money has Dubliners flocking to Parnell Street.

With over 100 types of noodles, the lunchtime deals at **Charming Noodle** (no.105) are among the best in town, and **Hop House** (no.103), a fusion of Korean and Japanese cuisine, boasts a sake bar and mural-lined beer garden. Don't be put off by the relative step up in presentation; there are just as many Asians packing out these hotspots as there are Irish.

Just a stone's throw to the south is another cultural enclave – Italian, this time – set to change the city's dining habits: the Quartier Bloom. Mostly run by people from a single village in the Lombardy region, its epicentre, Bloom's Lane, is the vision of one developer with an obsession for all things Italian. Aperitivo platters from traditional trattorias such as **Enoteca delle Langhe** (p93) make it an oasis for foodies; factor in the neighbouring gelateria, and its courtyard is an ideal spot for an alfresco afternoon. You can choose from 23 wines by the glass at **La Taverna de Bacco**, and have a gander at the lane's centrepiece, a tongue-in-cheek mural based on Da Vinci's *Last Supper*, where local residents stand in for the apostles. It's as good a reminder as any that Dublin is changing.

Henry Street

DUBLIN BY AREA

seating, an unpretentious bunch of punters and friendly staff are its biggest attractions. If you fancy a quiet pint, this place will fit the bill very nicely indeed.

Pravda

35 Liffey Street Lower (874 0090/ www.pravda.ie). All cross-city buses/ Luas Jervis. **Open** 4-11.30pm Mon, Wed; 4pm-2.30am Thur, Fri; noon-2.30am Sat; 12.30-11pm Sun. **Bar**. **Map** p90 B3 ⑯

An abundance of Cyrillic script stencilled on the walls does not an authentic Russian bar make; but Pravda pulls off the ersatz Eastern European thing pretty well. The building is large and rambling, and the atmosphere is chilled during the day and vibrant at night. It's a particularly nice place for an afternoon hot toddy, with its view of the Ha'penny Bridge and the shoppers streaming past; but after 10pm the volume of the music will drown out your inner monologue. The place could do with a lick of paint.

Twisted Pepper

NEW *54 Middle Abbey Street (873 4800/www.bodytonicmusic.com). All cross-citybuses/Luas Abbey Street.* **Open** 8am-midnight Mon-Wed, Sun; 10am-2.30am Thur-Sat. **Bar**. **Map** p90 B3 ⑲

Fading style bar Traffic passed into the capable hands of hot promoters Bodytonic in late 2008, and now has four new spaces on Middle Abbey Street: a café, stage for live bands, basement for hot DJs and a kitchen serving all-day gourmet Irish breakfasts. It's likely to be one of the city's hottest newcomers.

Woolshed

Parnell Centre, Parnell Street at Capel Street (872 4325/www.woolshedbaa. com) All cross-city buses/Luas Jervis. **Open** noon-11.30pm Mon-Wed; noon-1am Thur, Fri, Sun; 10.30am-1am Sat. **Bar**. **Map** p90 A2 ⑳

This place proudly proclaims itself home from home for 'Aussies, Kiwis and Saffas'. Drinking pints, playing pool and watching sport on TV fill up the day, while at night bands of decidedly mixed quality line up to crank up the volume (on the basis, apparently, that if it can't be good, it might as well be loud). Nearly always fun, though.

Yamamori Sushi

38 Lower Ormond Quay (872 0003/ www.yamamorisushi.ie). All cross-city buses/Luas Jervis. **Open** 12.15-11pm Mon-Wed, Sun; 12.15-11.30pm Thur-Sat. **€€€. Japanese. Map** p90 B3 ㉑
A lot more spacious than it appears from its unassuming entrance, Yamamori Sushi stretches back into a light, bright atrium with a busy sushi counter and rows of packed tables waited on by efficient business-like staff. The sushi here (nigiri and norimaki) is excellent – the best in the city, in fact – but there's plenty more on offer for those who'd rather have something hot or, at the very least, cooked. Try the richly flavoured salmon teriyaki or the hearty suki yaki (thinly sliced marbled sirloin served in a cast-iron pan).

Shopping

Arnotts

12 Henry Street (805 0400/www. arnotts.ie). All cross-city buses/Luas Jervis. **Open** 9am-6.30pm Mon, Wed, Fri, Sat; 9.30am-6.30pm Tue; 9am-9pm Thur; noon-6pm Sun. **Map** p90 B3 ㉒
Once an uninspiring department store better known for school uniforms than stylish clothing, Arnotts has completely reinvented itself as a vast and gleamingly modern department store.

Clery & Co

18-27 Lower O'Connell Street (878 6000/www.clerys.com). All cross-city buses/Luas Abbey Street. **Open** 9am-7pm Mon-Wed; 9am-9pm Thur; 9am-8pm Fri; 9am-6.30pm Sat; noon-6pm Sun. **Map** p90 B3 ㉓
Despite an auspicious beginning (it was one of the first purpose-built department stores in the world when it was founded in 1853), Clery & Co has long since been overtaken by its swisher, more modern competitors.

But, that said, its elegant premises (the wonderful old staircases, in particular) still exude a traditional charm and its decent selection of menswear (Kangol, Wrangler, YSL) and womenswear (Karen Millen, Miss Selfridge, Sisley, Topshop) keeps it in the race.

Dunnes Stores

Henry Street (872 3911/www.dunnes stores.ie). All cross-city buses/Luas Jervis. **Open** 9am-7pm Mon-Wed, Fri, Sat; 9am-9pm Thur; 11am-7pm Sun. **Map** p90 B3 ㉔
The ubiquitous Dunnes Stores holds a special place in the hearts of Dubliners, thanks to its good-value, no-nonsense gear. It's exceptionally inexpensive, carries a good range of babies' and children's clothes, and is great for well-priced home entertainment gear and homewares that can be surprisingly stylish. Some of the larger stores (such as this one) also sell groceries.

ILAC Shopping Centre

Henry Street (704 1460). All cross-city buses/Luas Jervis. **Open** 9am-6pm Mon-Wed, Fri, Sat; 9am-9pm Thur; noon-6pm Sun. **Map** p90 B3 ㉕
There was a time when the ILAC Centre was a byword for urban tawdriness, devoid of any charm, bereft of shops you'd actually want to set foot in. But those days are over. Extensive refurbishment and revamping of the centre has left it looking every bit the 21st-century mall.

Jen Kelly

50 North Great George's Street (874 5983). All cross-city buses. **Open** 8am-5.30pm Mon-Thur; 8am-4pm Fri. **Map** p90 B1 ㉖
Not somewhere you can just wander into, couturier Jen Kelly's exclusive studio is geared more to those with the budget and ideas for a bespoke service. His opulent creations are famed for their rich use of velvet, fur, satin and Chantilly lace, and while they may be costly, they are worth every penny. All work is carried out on these elegant Georgian premises.

DUBLIN BY AREA

Free wheelin'

Go for a spin in the city's newest – and cheapest – public transport.

Futuristic, bug-like vehicles have been seen on Dublin's roads. But there's no cause for alarm: they're here to help – and they don't cost a cent. Just when your weary legs are failing you, these helpful conveyances pull up and ask if you need a lift, free of charge.

Since their 2007 launch, the **Eco Cabs** (www.ecocabs.ie) have become a familiar part of the city landscape. These three-wheeled, open-sided cabs are essentially high-tech rickshaws, with seating in the back for two people, and extra propulsion from an electric motor to give the driver a boost when his pedalling power runs low.

The cabs are free because they are sponsored by a variety of companies that use the cab as a mobile billboard, but it's still standard practice to tip your driver. Hitch a ride at one of the six main pick up points: the Spire Island on O'Connell Street, St Stephen's Green Shopping Centre, the bottom of Grafton Street opposite the Molly Malone Statue, outside the Dublin Tourism Office on Suffolk Street, the Central bank on Dame Street, or the IFSC. They operate between 10am and 7pm and travel within a two-kilometre (1.2-mile) radius of the city centre. Later at night, ordinary pedal-powered rickshaws operate – for a fee – around the centre of town.

DUBLIN BY AREA

Jervis Centre

Jervis Street (878 1323/www.jervis.ie). All cross-city buses/Luas Jervis. **Open** 9am-6.30pm Mon-Wed; 9am-9pm Thur; 9am-7pm Fri, Sat; 11am-6.30pm Sun. **Map** p90 A3 ㉗

This starkly modern shopping centre may not be the most relaxing place in the world (crowds are a permanent fixture) but it is handily located, and it's also full of equally handy, bite-sized outlets. You'll find branches of big UK stores like Argos, Debenhams and M&S, plus a fair selection of clothes shops (Topshop and Next) and dozens of mall staples, of the Sunglass Hut and Boots varieties.

Winding Stair

40 Lower Ormond Quay (872 6576/ www.winding-stair.com). All cross-city buses/Luas Jervis. **Open** noon-5pm Tue-Sun. **Map** p90 B3 ㉘

You'll find plenty of interesting titles at this beguilingly quirky bookshop, where chandeliers hang from the ceiling and wing-backed armchairs face each other across a coffee table piled high with perusable volumes. And sometimes there'll even be music from the ancient record player to keep you company as you browse the shelves of classic and contemporary fiction, design texts and imaginative children's books. The restaurant, next door, is one of the capital's most popular restaurants, with a reputation for putting well-sourced, high-quality ingredients to imaginatively good use.

Woollen Mills

41 Lower Ormond Quay (828 0301). All cross-city buses/Luas Jervis. **Open** 9am-6pm Mon-Wed, Fri; 9am-7pm Thur; 9.30am-6pm Sat. **Map** p90 B3 ㉙

Spinning out the knitwear thang with considerable energy, the Mills has been going strong for well over a century now. Aran, cashmere, merino and mohair items are in plentiful supply, taking the form of sweaters, capes, scarves and cardies. Not exactly cutting edge but not dowdy, either.

Nightlife

Academy

57 Abbey Street Middle (877 9999 /www.theacademydublin.com). All cross-city buses/Luas Abbey Street. **Open** times vary. **Admission** prices vary. **Map** p90 B3 ③⓪

Formerly Spirit nightclub, the new-look Academy has been reborn largely as a live venue. Still, there is much to love here for clubbers: ditching the complacent vibe that befell its naff predecessor, the Academy comes to life on Saturday nights. Spinning current club favourites and festival tracks, popular DJs including FM104 DJ Al Gibbs are on hand to provide the ultimate Saturday night soundtrack. Think CSS and Klaxons rubbing proverbial shoulders with Felix da Housecat and Roger Sanchez.

Ambassador

Top of O'Connell Street (0818 719 300/www.mcd.ie/venues). All cross-city buses/Luas Abbey Street. **Open** times vary. **Admission** prices vary. **Map** p90 B2 ③①

The Ambassador was a theatre, then a woefully underused cinema. As a rock venue, it keeps many of its old trappings: decor, balcony and a large stage. It's a big stage to fill, and it takes loud rock bands like the Queens of the Stone Age or charismatic indie acts like Beck to put the place to best use. The management has pretty much cornered the Dublin market in nu metal and hard indie rock; an acoustic act would be lost in this 1,200-seat venue.

Hugh Lane

Parnell Square North (222 5550/www. hughlane.ie). Bus 3, 10, 11, 13, 16, 19, 46A, 48A/Luas Abbey Street. **Open** 10am-6pm Tue-Thur; 10am-5pm Fri, Sat; 11am-5pm Sun. **Admission** free. **Map** p90 B1 ③②

This ample hall in the Hugh Lane Gallery hosts the long-running and stylish Sunday at Noon concerts. The hour-long series features jazz, contemporary and classical music from Ireland and abroad, and runs from October to June.

Gate p101

DUBLIN BY AREA

Savoy

Around 30 concerts a year, funded by Dublin City Council and the Arts Council, are performed.

Pravda
35 Liffey Street Lower (874 0090/www.pravda.ie). All cross-city buses/Luas Jervis. **Open** 4-11.30pm Mon, Wed; 4pm-2.30am Thur, Fri; noon-2.30am Sat; 12.30-11pm Sun. **Admission** free. **Map** p90 B3 ③③
One of the more consistent spots on the north side of Dublin's River Liffey, this Russian-themed bar has comfy seating and a fine selection of vodkas, all surrounded by Soviet iconography. The bar hosts numerous music nights from funk to live bands. Thursday's riotous King Kong Club is arguably the high point in Pravda's week, teeming as it is with gorgeous, fun-loving young things.

Arts & leisure

Abbey
26 Abbey Street Lower (box office 878 7222/www.abbeytheatre.ie). All cross-city buses/Luas Abbey Street. **Tickets** €20-€30; €14-15 reductions (Mon-Fri). **Map** p90 C3 ③④

Internationally renowned theatre designer Jean-Guy Lecat has transformed the auditorium of this, the nation's premier theatre. Where there used to be a balcony there is now elegantly sloping seating, with no awkward corners left for bad sightlines and dodgy sound. And while plans for its move to Docklands have been finalised, the actual realities of transposing the Abbey to its new location were, at the time of writing, far from looming on the horizon.

Cineworld
Parnell Centre, Parnell Street (872 8895/www.cineworld.ie). All cross-city buses. **Tickets** €8-€10; €6-€8 reductions; €25-€28.40 family. **Map** p90 A2 ③⑤
Since it opened about a decade ago, this multiplex has been through more names than Prince (Virgin, UGC) but through each name change, it has remained exactly the same: the latest releases on the best screens, crystal-clear sound, chairs you can fall asleep in and super-sized tubs of popcorn. Be sure to book or come well in advance.

Gate

1 Cavendish Row, Parnell Square (874 4045/www.gate-theatre.ie). All cross-city buses/Luas Abbey Street. **Tickets** €27-€35. **Map** p90 B2 ③⑥

The Abbey theatre's misfortune is the Gate's opportunity. While the national theatre of Ireland has been foundering since the start of the millennium, its younger, sassier rival has gone from strength to strength. The Gate's director, Michael Colgan, runs a shrewd operation, mixing international stars with local greats in quality productions that have theatregoers queuing for returns. He's helped by having the most elegant, spacious theatre in the city (which was being further improved with the construction of a new €5.2 million wing at the time of writing) and by a rambunctious, cosmopolitan legacy.

Hillsboro Gallery

49 Parnell Square West (878 8242/ www.hillsborofineart.com). All cross-city buses/Luas Abbey Street. **Open** 10.30am-6pm Mon-Fri; 10.30am-4pm Sat. No credit cards. **Map** p90 B2 ③⑦

Just around the corner from the Hugh Lane Gallery (p91), the Hillsboro Gallery is beautifully situated in a restored Georgian townhouse. It specialises in contemporary Irish, American and European art, with various works by the 'St Ives artists' (William Scott, Nancy Wynne Jones and others) and paintings by Kenneth Noland and Larry Poons, among many, many others.

Savoy

16-17 O'Connell Street Upper (0818 776 776/www.savoy.ie). All cross-city buses/Luas Abbey Street **Tickets** €9; €6-€8 reductions. **Map** p90 B2 ③⑧

The Savoy, long a fixture of shabby 1970s chic that perfectly complemented the litter-strewn O'Connell Street has, finally had its face-lift. These days, it's in a timewarp of wood panelling and fake chandeliers, and has gone from atmospheric to anodyne, but the seats are definitely more comfortable and the box office more responsive, so many will accept the trade-off. Expect the usual mainstream blockbuster and rom-com programming.

Old Jameson Distillery p104

The North Quays & Around

DUBLIN BY AREA

The North Quays is the collective name for the series of streets that run to the west of Docklands' Custom House along the northern embankment of the Liffey. Although it appears as one long street, the names change every block or so – Eden Quay, Bachelors Walk, Ormond Quay, Inns Quay – as do the individual characters of the discrete residential hubs that are scattered along this mile-long stretch. There are also several markets, including the remnants of the fabled Smithfield horse-trading fair, and the city's biggest green space (**Phoenix Park**) to be explored. It's busy, bustling and fascinating, and well worth your time.

Sights & museums

Dublin Zoo
Phoenix Park (474 8900/www.dublin zoo.ie). Bus 10, 25, 25A, 26, 51, 66, 67, 68, 69. **Open** *Jan* 9.30am-4.30pm Mon-Sat; 10.30am-4.30pm Sun. *Feb* 9.30am-5pm Mon-Sat; 10.30am-5pm Sun. *Mar* 9.30am-6pm Mon-Sat; 10.30am-6pm Sun. *Apr-Sept* 9.30am-6.30pm Mon-Sat; 10.30am-6.30pm Sun. *Oct* 9.30am-5.30pm Mon-Sat; 9.30am-5.30pm Sun. *Nov-Dec* 9.30am-4pm Mon-Sat; 10.30am-4pm Sun. **Admission** €14.50; €5.20-€12 reductions; €42-€50 family; free under-3s. **Map** p104 A1 ❶
One of the oldest zoos in the world (founded in 1830), Dublin's animal house is now home to 700 species, including endangered snow leopards and golden lion tamarinds. In terms of layout it is the epitome of a modern,

eco-conscious facility, with tigers, elephants, chimps and hundreds more given all the time and space they need to feel (climate notwithstanding) right at home. The place is also run with children very much in mind, as proved by the Pets' Corner, the Zoo Train, and the ample picnic facilities and play areas. That said, though, it's far from miniature in scale: the impressive Asian Plains, for example, is a 32-acre (13-hectare) expanse of pasture and woodland, home to (among many others) some splendid white rhinos and the ever-expanding family of elephants. All in all, then, this is an excellent day out – just one word of warning: try to turn up as near to opening time as possible, as queues can be long and (especially for the junior contingent) joyless.

National Museum of Ireland: Decorative Arts & History

Collins Barracks, Benburb Street (677 7444/www.museum.ie). Bus 25, 25A, 37, 39, 66, 67, 90, 172/Luas Museum.

Open 10am-5pm Tue-Sat; 2-5pm Sun.
Admission free. Map p104 C1 ②

Housed in the breathtaking confines of the barracks formerly used by the British Army, this museum contains the nation's most significant collection of decorative arts, as well as myriad displays devoted to Ireland's social, political and military histories. All of the exhibitions are complemented by informative, interactive multimedia displays, and are frequently supplemented by workshops and talks. The Earth Science Museum contains geological collections, fossils and even the odd chunk of dinosaur – kept well away from the china. There's also an excellent permanent exhibition about the influential Irish designer Eileen Gray, which is excellent and well worth a look. But the latest, and arguably most involving, addition to the museum is the 'Soldiers and Chiefs' exhibition, which artfully documents the impact of four and a half centuries of warfare on the ordinary Irishman. The museum's website is a good source of events information.

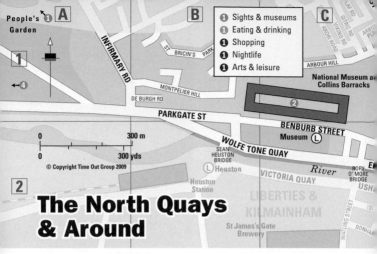

People's
Garden

	Sights & museums
	Eating & drinking
	Shopping
	Nightlife
	Arts & leisure

National Museum a
Collins Barracks

PARKGATE ST

BENBURB STREET
Museum Ⓛ

WOLFE TONE QUAY

SEAN
HEUSTON
BRIDGE

Ⓛ Heuston

VICTORIA QUAY

River

RORY
O' MORE
BRIDGE

0   300 m
0   300 yds

© Copyright Time Out Group 2009

Heuston
Station

LIBERTIES &
KILMAINHAM

St James's Gate
Brewery

The North Quays
& Around

Old Jameson Distillery

*Bow Street, Smithfield Village (807
2355/www.oldjamesondistillery.com).
Bus 25, 26, 37, 39, 67, 67A, 68, 69,
79/Luas Smithfield.* **Open** 9.30am-6pm
(last tour 5.30pm) daily. **Admission**
(by guided tour only) €12.50; €6-€9
reductions; €25 family.
Map p105 D2 ❸

Providing a hard-stuff counterpoint to
the Guinness Storehouse, Dublin's
other big alcohol-tied tourist attraction,
the Old Jameson Distillery does its best
to sell visitors on the cultural mythol-
ogy behind John Jameson's fabled
whiskey (always, in this case, spelt
with an 'e'). Highlights include beautifully crafted models of distillery ves-
sels. The tours could delve a little
deeper, but at least you'll get to taste
some of the stuff at the end.

Phoenix Park Visitors'
Centre

*Phoenix Park (677 0095/www.heritage
ireland.ie). Bus 37, 39.* **Open** *Mid Mar-
Sept* 10am-6pm daily. *Oct* 10am-5.30pm
daily. *Nov-mid Mar* 10am-6pm Mon-
Wed, Sat, Sun. **Admission** free.
Map p104 A1 ❹

Housed in the old coach house of the
former Papal Nunciature, this centre

explains the history of Phoenix Park.
Regular free tours of nearby Ashtown
Castle, a 17th-century tower house,
are offered, and tours to Aras
an Uachtarain, a Palladian lodge that
is the President of Ireland's official
residence, also depart from the centre
on Saturdays throughout the year.
For tour times and availability, call
677 7129.

St Michan's Church

*Church Street Lower (872 4154).
Bus 25, 26, 37, 39, 67, 67A, 68, 69,
79/Luas Four Courts/Smithfield.* **Open**
Mid Mar-Oct 10am-12.45pm, 2-4.45pm
Mon-Fri; 10am-12.45pm Sat. *Nov-mid
Mar* 12.30-3.30pm Mon-Fri; 10am-
12.45pm Sat. **Admission** €4;
€3-€3.50 reductions. No credit cards.
Map p105 E2 ❺

There has been a place of worship on
this site since 1096, and the current
building dates from 1686, though it
was drastically restored in 1828 and
again following the Civil War. Those
with an interest in the macabre will
love the 17th-century vaults composed
of magnesium limestone, where mummified bodies – including a crusader, a
nun and a suspected thief – have rest-
ed for centuries showing no signs of

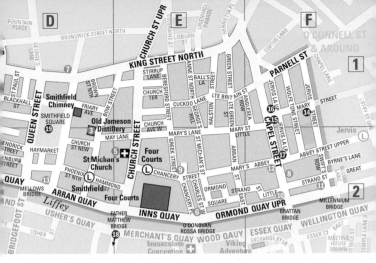

decomposition. You used to be able to touch one of the mummy's hands, and indeed sometimes still can if the guide is in a good mood.

Eating & drinking

Chancery

1 Inns Quay (677 0420). All cross-city buses/Luas Four Courts. **Open** 7.30am-11.30pm Mon-Sat; noon-11pm Sun. No credit cards. **Pub**. **Map** p105 E2

At first glance, the Chancery is a spit-and-sawdust local with little to recommend it. It is, however, worthy of note as one of Dublin's early houses – bars that are legally allowed to open at 7.30am. For that reason, it's a popular final port of call for clubbers. It can be an odd (some would say dispiriting) experience to enter a bar so early and find people behaving as if it were the top of Saturday night, but it's certainly worth knowing about.

Cobblestone

77 King Street North (872 1799/ www.imro.ie). Bus 25, 26, 37, 39, 67, 67A, 68, 69, 79/Luas Smithfield. **Open** 4-11.30pm Mon-Thur; 4pm-12.30am Fri, Sat; 1-11pm Sun. No credit cards. **Pub**. **Map** p105 D1

The musicians' corner downstairs attracts traditional players whom you would pay to see elsewhere, and the paying venue upstairs rarely books a duff band (lo-fi, trad and folk tend to dominate). Overall it's cosy, while eschewing unnecessary frills; if you want to avoid excessive paddywhackery in favour of genuine traditional Dublin pubbery, come here.

Gospoda Polska

NEW *15 Capel Street (874 9394/ www.gospodapolska.ie). All cross-city buses/Luas Jervis.* **Open** noon-10pm Mon-Thur; noon-11.30pm Fri, Sat; 12.30-10pm Sun. **€€€**. **Polish**. **Map** p105 F2

A welcome breath of fresh air on a stretch of Capel Street that is otherwise given over to sex shops and tatty boutiques, this smart new Polish restaurant is a cosy and quietly chic little outfit. Simple wooden furniture and discreetly patterned wallpaper are glammed up by the addition of a few chandeliers, while the menu pulls off a similar trick by offering traditional rustic grub alongside some snappier lunchtime options (paninis, salads and the like). But the predominant appeal of a place like this is

National Museum p103

the chance it offers to carb up on comfort food like 'hunting style' pork chops, potato cakes and big bowls of deliciously chunky soup, all washed down with gallons of crisp, strong lager.

Hughes' Bar
19 Chancery Street, off Church Street (872 6540). All cross-city buses/Luas Four Courts. **Open** 7am-11.30pm Mon-Thur; 7am-12.30am Fri, Sat; 7-11pm Sun. **Pub**. Map p105 E2 ⑨
Hughes sits next to the law courts. Some argue there's a rough edge to it, but its excellent trad music sessions make it worth a visit. Actor Brendan Gleeson pops in from time to time and Bob Dylan's backing band joined the house musicians recently for the type of unplanned and informal gig for which the pub is becoming known.

Jack Nealons
165 Capel Street (872 3247). All cross-city buses Luas Jervis. **Open** noon-11.30pm Mon-Thur, Sun; noon-12.30am Fri, Sat. **Bar**. Map p105 F2 ⑩
Popular with pre-clubbers, Nealons is stylish but relaxed. The downstairs bar is usually less hectic than upstairs, but at weekends you take a seat where you can find it. If the drinks seem slightly on the pricey side, the happily braying customers don't object. Look out for the juggling barmen, whose cocktail expertise may tempt you towards something more adventurous than a pint of plain.

Morrison Hotel Bar
Morrison Hotel, Ormond Quay Lower (887 2400/www.morrisonhotel.ie). All cross-city buses/Luas Jervis. **Open** 10.30am-11.30pm Mon-Thur; 10.30am-12.30am Fri, Sat; noon-11.30pm Sun. **Bar**. Map p105 F2 ⑪
This place is pure class. With an interior designed by fashion guru John Rocha, the Morrison's extremely stylish bar has plenty of comfy black couches on which you can sip cocktails and dreamily peer out at the silvery Liffey mist. What's particularly good about the place is its combination of the aforementioned quality with some

Baby boom

The animals went in two by two – and you can guess what happened next.

2008 was a bumper year for **Dublin Zoo** (p102). Its roll call of animals was lengthened by the birth of an elephant, a giraffe, a rare white rhino, a sea lion and a Brazilian tapir – not to mention the dozen flamenco chicks currently waddling around the place, or the female gorilla and second female giraffe expected to give birth just as this guide went to press.

All these new arrivals have attracted unprecedented numbers of visitors. Families have flocked to see baby elephant Budi play with her one-year-old cousin, and to marvel at the little white rhino, Zukiswa, the first rhino born in Dublin in 14 years – said to run around so fast it's as though she's wound up on a spring. Feeding time for the baby giraffe has also been a draw, with crowds watching zookeepers teeter at the top of ladders to feed her bottles of milk. (She's being reared by the

zookeepers because her mother rejected her shortly after her birth.)

With so many endearing new residents, and a long list of established ones, there's plenty to see; the zoo covers 60 acres, so there's a lot of ground to cover too. Happily, the zoo is very well organised, so it's easy to pick and choose your favourite beasts if time is short. A map at the entrance, which you can also download from the zoo's website, clearly shows where all the animals reside and how to get to them.

The zoo is divided into two parts – the African Plains safari area, which you take a trailer around, and the main area, which you can explore on foot. In Easter 2009 the zoo launches a new area called African Savana, which will let people get much closer to the hippos, giraffes, zebras, tigers and lions.

Light House

of the friendliest bar staff in the city. If you've got the cash, there's truly no more salubrious spot at which to spend an evening. Dress to impress and arrive early.

Rhodes D7

The Capel Building, Mary Abbey (1-890 277 777 804 444/www.rhodesd7.com). All cross-city buses/Luas Jervis. **Open** noon-10pm Tue-Sat. **€€€. European.** **Map** p105 F2 ⑫

The Spiky Haired One has put his name to this large and buzzy 250-seater, but you won't find him at the stove. This brasserie is an exercise in branding only, with Rhodes's head chef Paul Hargreaves running the operation. The menu is sensibly priced and gently appealing: salmon fishcakes with a smoked salmon, lemon and dill butter sauce; slow roast pork belly with apple, apricot, onion and sage tart tatin – that kind of thing. Expect a battalion of staff, plasma screens, a thumping piano and an outdoor terrace for smokers. Lunchtimes are busy with Ireland's finest lawyers; dinner, though, attracts large, noisy groups looking for pleasant food that won't break the bank.

Voodoo Lounge

39 Arran Quay (873 6013). All cross-city buses/Luas Smithfield. **Open** noon-1am Mon-Wed; noon-2.30am Thur, Fri; 4pm-3am Sat; 4pm-1am Sun. No credit cards. **Bar/club. Map** p105 D2 ⑬

Voodoo is a happening bar-club with garage bands seven nights a week and DJs at weekends. (A board in the window communicates the musical line-up.) Inside, the masks, beads and other scary paraphernalia are dimly lit by candles and complemented by eerie murals on supernatural themes. Happily, the likeable staff ensure that the vibe remains positive. Plenty of bottled beers, yummy pizza slices and an old Space Invader machine make it worth trekking up the quays for a bit of black magic.

Shopping

Banba Toymaster

48 Mary Street, (872 7100). All cross-city buses/Luas Jervis. **Open** 9.30am-6pm Mon-Wed, Fri, Sat; 9.30am-8pm Thur; noon-6pm Sun. **Map** p105 F1 ⑭

The young and young-at-heart are likely to lose their heads in this

DUBLIN BY AREA

colossal pantheon of play. The tightly packed aisles roar with every big brand name you can think of, as kids cluster around the latest toys.

Louis Copeland

39-41 Capel Street (872 1600/ www.louiscopeland.com). All cross-city buses/Luas Jervis. **Open** 9am-6pm Mon-Wed, Fri, Sat; 9am-8pm Thur. **Map** p105 F1 ⑮

Ireland's most famous tailor has been kitting out the chaps for over a century. As well as Copeland's own brand, the store also stocks suits from Hugo Boss, Armani and Canali.

Millets Camping

61 Mary Street (873 3571). All cross-city buses/Luas Jervis. **Open** 9am-6pm Mon-Wed, Fri, Sat; 9am-7.30pm Thur; noon-6pm Sun. Map p105 F1 ⑯

This Millets (no, not the other one) will kit you out for any expedition. Travellers with serious adventure intent should make their way through the door of this Mary Street institution for high-quality tents, camping equipment, and durable, waterproof footwear. Discounts are possible for those who belong to the MCI, a body representing climbers and walkers.

Nightlife

PantiBar

7-8 Capel Street (874 0710/ www.pantibar.com). All cross-city buses/Luas Jervis. **Open** 5-11.30pm Mon, Wed, Sun; 5pm-2am Tue; 5pm-2.30am Thur; Fri, Sat. **Map** p105 F2 ⑰

This is a new-school gay bar – which means, apparently, that you can't really tell that it's a gay bar: PantiBar is more about postmodern interior design than camp and cross-dressing. As with most gay-friendly bars, the music is the best pop party tunes. Owned and run by Dublin's best-loved drag queen Panti, who takes to the stage for what is arguably the most popular drag show each Thursday. From intimate acoustic sessions to the intriguingly-titled 'Furry Glen Bear Nights', there is something on Pantibar's slate for everyone.

Vicar Street

99 Vicar Street, off Thomas Street West (454 5533/www.vicarstreet.com). Bus 123. **Open** *Live music* from 7.30pm daily. **Map** p105 E2 ⑱

A modern venue with an old-style feel, Vicar Street has comfortable seating, sensitive lighting and a great sound system. It was recently expanded to hold 1,000 punters, but has lost none of its intimate atmosphere. The spacious pub in the front and the little bars hidden in the corridors are handy, too. Acts include Bob Dylan, Kanye West, Rufus Wainwright, Calexico and Al Green, as well as big-name jazz and comedy acts and top local musicians.

Arts & Leisure

Light House

Market Square, off Smithfield Square, (879 7601/www.lighthousecinema.ie). All cross-city buses/Luas Smithfield. **Map** p105 D1 ⑲

Foreign-language and art-house movies reign supreme at this welcome addition to the city's independent cinema scene. The theatres here are probably the most comfortable (and certainly the most stylish) in town.

DUBLIN BY AREA

St George's Dock

Docklands

Spanning 1,300 acres (520 hectares) of land on the northern and southern banks of the River Liffey, Dublin's Docklands were, until recently, languishing in a semi-derelict state and suffering from low employment. But all that changed when the Dublin Docklands Development Authority was created in 1997; now, after more than a decade of work, the area has been transformed. Smart office blocks, restaurants, wine bars and pubs have all flung open their doors in recent years.

But what makes Dublin's dockside regeneration differ from similar projects across Europe is the emphasis that has been placed on quality of design: some of the most famous architects in the world have already begun or

are due to start work on a variety of ambitious projects. All of which means that, in a city of historic charms, this riverside neighbourhood provides a refreshing glimpse into the future of an ever-evolving skyline.

Sights & museums

Custom House Visitor Centre

Custom House Quay (888 2538). Bus 53A, 90A/Luas Busáras/DART Tara Street. **Open** *Mid Mar-Nov* 10am-12.30pm, 2-5pm Mon-Fri; 2-5pm Sat, Sun. *Dec-mid Mar* 10am-12.30pm, 2-5pm Wed-Fri. **Admission** €1.50; €4 family. **Map** p111 A1 ❶
This small, unsophisticated centre offers access only to a small area of the building (in and around the domed

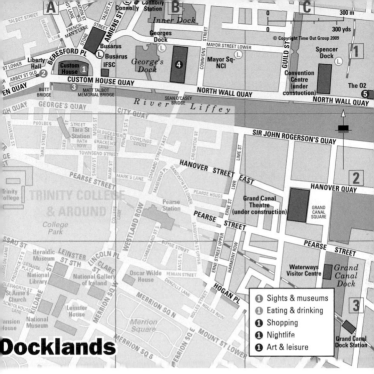

Docklands

1 Sights & museums
1 Eating & drinking
1 Shopping
1 Nightlife
1 Art & leisure

Clock Tower) but it is definitely worth a visit, if only for the extra perspective it gives on the building's elaborate and (for its time) extraordinary architectural features. Displays and a video relate the history of the building and its intrepid, dedicated architect James Gandon.

Liberty Hall

33 Eden Quay (874 9731/www. libertyhall.ie). Bus 53A, 90A/Luas Busárus/DART Tara Street. **Open** times vary. **Admission** prices vary. **Map** p111 A1 **2**

Dublin's tallest building and the current headquarters of the Services, Industrial, Professional and Technical Union (SIPTU), Liberty Hall has a colourful past. The first building to be constructed on this site (not the one

you see now, which was built in the 1960s following the demolition of the original) dated back to the beginning of the last century, and played a dramatic part in many of the landmark events of Dublin's modern history. At various times, Liberty Hall was used as the headquarters of Jim Larkin's Irish Transport and General Workers Union, the base of operations for James Connolly, a printing house for the Irish Worker and an arms and munitions production line for the 1916 Easter Rising. The building itself is not open to visitors, but the Liberty Hall Centre next door, which programmes a wide variety of musical and cultural events, is always worth a snoop around.

Electric docks

There's a growing buzz at the water's edge.

For all the hype whipped up around Dublin's Docklands, the area still all but dies once the office workers have trooped out for the weekend. As this book went to press, only the recently revamped **chq** complex (p114) – home to attractive retail units such as furniture store Meadows & Byrne, and pleasant refreshment stops like the cosy wine bar Ely – provided much in the way of incentive to linger.

But things will get better – much better, and fast. The purely aesthetic side of things is being taken care of by some of the world's top architects, names like Manuel Aires Mateus, who has produced a five-star hotel that will open in 2009; and Santiago Calatrava, whose Beckett Bridge, the curved profile of which resembles a harp laid on its side, is currently under construction.

Other improvements go well below the surface. A concerted effort is being made to bring the arts to the Docklands, and in particular to make use of its attractive squares and outdoor spaces. Luvvies are aflutter at the prospect that the National Theatre (currently located on Abbey Street) will find a new dockside home with the capacity to seat 1,000 people. And then there's the vast music venue formerly known as the Point Theatre, which was drab and suffered from poor sound and sight lines; now revamped and given a new name – **02** (p114) – it's bound be a vast improvement.

As a harbinger of the Docklands' rise to artistic prominence, several shows on the 2008 fringe festival programme took place here, and July's Analog festival, which drew in acts such as Teddy Thompson and Lou Reed, brought a party vibe to Grand Canal Square. What's more, just prior to that earful, Docklands residents had an eyeful, when artist Spencer Tunick invited 2,500 members of the public to bare all for a photograph. Mass nudity is a tricky cultural symptom to interpret – but like many other things around here, it certainly couldn't have been imagined a few years ago.

Custom House p110

Jeanie Johnston

Custom House Quay (066 712 9999/ www.jeaniejohnston.ie). Bus 53A, 90A/Luas Busáras/DART Tara Street. **Open** *10.30am-5pm Sat, Sun.* **Admission** *Museum €5.* **Map** p111 A1 ❸

Only in town at certain times of the year (the winter season is usually a pretty safe bet), the *Jeanie Johnston* is a working replica of Dublin's most famous famine ship (the boats that were used in the mid 19th century to transport victims of the famine to a brighter, better life abroad). The famine ships earned the grim nickname of 'floating coffins' due to the mortality rate of their frail and disease-ravaged passengers, but the JJ was a notable exception: despite carrying around 2,500 people on 16 separate voyages to America, she never lost a single soul. This remarkable feat, along with the blighted period of Ireland's history that made it necessary, are the subjects of a small museum located inside the ship. Using data from the Lloyd's Survey, this replica vessel was painstakingly produced, timber for timber, to match the original, and upon completion in 2003 was broken in with a voyage to America, stopping at 20 ports in five countries along the way.

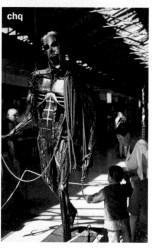

chq

Shopping

chq

Custom House Quay, Docklands (673 6054/www.chq.ie). All cross-city buses/ Luas Busáras/DART Connolly. **Open** *7am-7pm Mon-Fri; 10am-6pm Sat; noon-6pm Sun.* **Map** p111 B1 ❹

Not only is it impressive to look at (the building was formerly a John Rennie-designed tobacco warehouse) but this sleek new shopping centre is perfectly suited to Docklands' upwardly mobile demographics. Smart, glass-fronted retail units stock everything from designer homewares (Meadows & Byrne) and upmarket gents' threads (Henry Jermyn) to chic womenswear (Kohl, Pink Room, Fran & Jane) and speciality teas (House of Tea). There's also the usual clutch of coffeeshops.

Nightlife

O2

NEW *East Link Bridge, North Wall Quay, (general enquiries 676 6144/ www.theo2.ie). Tara Street or Connolly DART/rail.* **Map** p111 C1 ❺

Dublin's largest indoor music venue has had a massive overhaul, and opens in December 2008 with the new name O2. It will have a 14,000 capacity arena, 2,000-seater theatre, hotel, shopping centre and underground car park.

Kilmainham Gaol p117

The Liberties & Kilmainham

The tour buses sweep through, stopping only at the key attractions as they loop back round into the town centre, but it's worth spending a little time getting to know this frequently overlooked part of the city. This is, after all, where the black stuff was made and where many a rebel came undone.

Just beyond Christ Church, the Liberties (so called because it was a self-governing area beyond what were the city limits) is one of the oldest and liveliest districts of Dublin. Its markets, the vibrancy of the street life on its main artery, Thomas Street, and its association with the Guinness family all lend

it character – yet it remains among the most disadvantaged areas of the city. Fortunately, it has been marked out for redevelopment as Dublin's new Soho; but it's also where you'll find a seam of atmospheric, dusty and interesting antiques stores.

Heading west from the Guinness brewery, you come to the Kilmainham district. Whereas the Liberties epitomises Dublin at its most urban, Kilmainham offers a very different experience. The area is distinctly 'villagey'; the semi-rural ambience is helped by the amount of green space as well as the views across the river to the vast expanse of Phoenix Park.

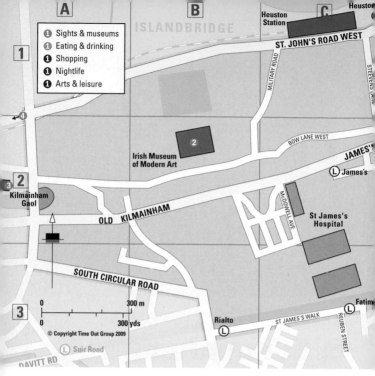

Sights & museums

Guinness Storehouse

St James's Gate (408 4800/www. guinness-storehouse.com). Bus 51B, 78A, 123/Luas James's Street. **Open** *Sept-June 9.30am-5pm daily. July, Aug 9.30am-7pm daily.* **Admission** €15; €8-€10 reductions; €30 family; free under-6s. **Map** p117 D2 **1**

It may no longer be part of the active brewery but this 'visitor experience', housed in a six-storey listed building dating from 1904, has become the popular public face of what is undoubtedly Ireland's most recognisable brand. The building is designed around a pint glass-shaped atrium and incorporates a retail store, exhibition space, function rooms, a restaurant and two bars. Much of the vast floor space is taken up with presentations on the history and making of the humble pint, which, although self-congratulatory in tone, are magnificently realised. Most entertaining, perhaps, is the advertising section – a testament to the company's famously imaginative marketing. The tour includes a complimentary pint of the best Guinness you are likely to get, and there's nowhere better to drink it than the Gravity Bar (p120).

Irish Museum of Modern Art

Royal Hospital, Military Road (612 9900/www.imma.ie). Bus 51, 51B, 78A, 79, 90, 123/Luas James's or Heuston. **Open** *10am-5.30pm Tue, Thur-Sat; 10.30am-5.30pm Wed;*

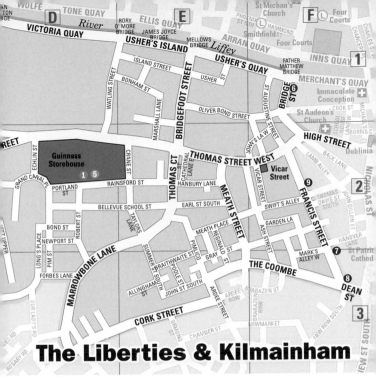

The Liberties & Kilmainham

noon-5.30pm Sun. **Admission** free. **Map** p116 B2 ❷

One of the most important 17th-century buildings in Ireland, the Royal Hospital was designed by Sir William Robinson in 1684 to serve as a nursing home for retired soldiers, and, famously, he modelled it on Les Invalides in Paris. It was founded by James Butler, Duke of Ormonde and Viceroy to King Charles II. In 1991 the place was reopened in the form of this modern art museum, with superb exhibition spaces distributed around its peaceful square. The displays are usually temporary shows, combined with a selection from a small permanent collection – a recent highlight was Carlos Amorales' mesmerising mix of haunting imagery and

evocative piano music, Dark Mirror. On the ground floor, the Heritage section provides some fascinating and (in the case of the Gallipoli accounts) occasionally horrifying background on the Royal Hospital and the pensioners who lived there. The grounds include a beautifully restored baroque formal garden, as well as Bully's Acre (one of the city's largest cemeteries, containing ancient burial sites and a military graveyard) and 19th-century stable buildings.

Kilmainham Gaol

Inchicore Road (453 5984/www. heritageireland.ie). Bus 51B, 51C, 78A, 79, 79a. **Open** (guided tour only) *Apr-Sept* 9.30am-5pm daily. *Oct-Mar* 9.30am-4pm Mon-Sat; 10am-5pm Sun.

Through a glass darkly

Guinness tales

There can be few images as iconic in the world of brewing as that of the swirling black-and-white cloudscape of a pint of Guinness settling in its glass. Even the name itself has become synonymous with a certain kind of twinkly-eyed nostalgia for the vanishing glory days of 'Old Dublin'.

But lurking behind the legend is a far more ordinary story of hard work, enterprise and a commitment to building an empire that has prospered for more than two and a half centuries.

In 1759, the founder of this Irish institution, Arthur Guinness, took out a 9,000-year lease on the St James's Gate brewery (the original document is still on display today). But the man who would go on to establish the huge Guinness fortune was, in fact, Arthur's great-grandson, Edward Cecil Guinness. Having bought out his brothers' shares in the brewery before he turned 30, Edward Cecil made Guinness a public company in 1886 (after he'd been made the first Earl of Iveagh), earning himself a vast personal fortune while still retaining more than 50 per cent of the shares. When he died in 1927 at the age of 80, his son Rupert took over as chairman, and was in turn succeeded by Benjamin Guinness, the third Earl of Iveagh, who died in 1992. As well as being head of the board at Guinness, Benjamin held the unique distinction of having been a senator, a member of the Oireachtas (Irish Parliament) and a member of the UK House of Lords.

Although the family holding in the company – now mostly owned by drinks behemoth Diageo – has been diluted to a mere three per cent, it is still enough to establish the family as the 26th richest in Britain. With over ten million pints being sold daily, some people's thirst for Guinness seems unquenchable.

The story of this family is living testament to the adage 'Guinness is good for you'.

Admission €5.30; €2.10-€3.70 reductions; €11.50 family.
Map p116 A2 ❸

Although it ceased to be used as a prison in 1924, this remains the best-known Irish lock-up, and one of the most fascinating buildings in the country. It was here that the leaders of the 1916 Easter Rising, along with many others, were executed. If you harbour an interest in the Rising or, indeed, any previous rebellions in Ireland from the 18th century onwards, you'll find Kilmainham Gaol a lot more informative and evocative than the National Museum. Multimedia displays documenting the atrocious prison conditions of the past are grimly informative, but it's the lively guided tours that steal the show. Groups are led through dank corridors, past bleak cells and into the evocative main hall (where some of the opening scenes of the original *Italian Job* were filmed). The sites of various executions, vigils, injustices and condemnations are conjured to vivid life, leaving you with a curious conflict of guilt and relief as you walk back out through the gates and into the free world.

War Memorial Gardens

Entrances: Con Colbert Road and South Circular Road, Islandbridge (888 3233/ www.heritageireland.ie/en/Dublin/War MemorialGardens). **Open** 8am-dusk Mon-Fri; 10am-dusk Sat, Sun.
Admission free. **Map** p116 A2 ❹

Designed by British architect Sir Edwin Lutyens as a tribute to the 49,400 Irish soldiers who died in World War I (each end of the grounds

Guinness Storehouse p120

DUBLIN BY AREA

is guarded by a granite bookroom containing manuscripts of the dead soldiers' names), these gardens retain an austere beauty. Covering eight hectares (20 acres) of the southern slopes of the River Liffey with granite columns, sunken circular rose gardens, pergolas, fountains and lily ponds, it is a masterfully landscaped space. But due to its slightly out-of-the-way location, few tend to bother with the journey up here, or indeed even seem to know of its existence, meaning that the gardens are rarely crowded. All of which is great news for the architecture buffs, clued-up tourists and local strollers who get the place all to themselves.

Eating & drinking

Gravity Bar

James Street (471 4527/www.guinness-storehouse. com). Bus 51B, 78A, 123/Luas James's Street. **Open** (admission with tour only) *Jan-Mar, Oct-Dec 9.30am-5pm daily. Apr-Sept 9.30am-7pm daily.* **Bar**. Map p117 D2 ❺

The Guinness Storehouse on James Street is one of the most popular tourist attractions in Dublin. Not surprising, considering the highlight of the tour is the experience offered by the Gravity Bar. Set at the top of a converted grain house, this very special bar commands a 360° view of Dublin from floor-to-ceiling windows. With the Guinness making the shortest journey in the world from vat to glass, the beer is great, too.

Nightlife

O'Shea's Merchant

12 Bridge Street Lower, Liberties (679 3797). Bus 21, 21A/Luas The Four Courts. **Open** *10.30am-11.30pm Mon-Wed; 10.30am-2am Thur-Sat; 12.30pm-2am Sun.* Map p117 F1 ❻

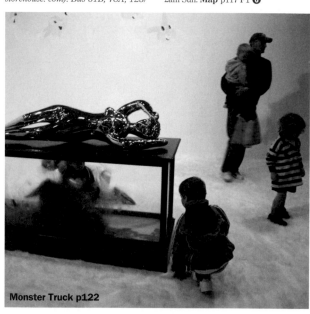

Monster Truck p122

Outside in

Dublin's modern art museum opens up.

Irish Museum of Modern Art p116

When it first opened, in the grounds of the 17th-century Royal Hospital Kilmainham in 1991, the **Irish Museum of Modern Art** (p116) drew criticism from people who felt that a city centre location would have been more likely to attract reluctant gallery-goers; but thanks to the recent introduction of the Luas red line, the museum is now eminently accessible. Under the aegis of current director Enrique Juncaso, it has also shaken off accusations of parochialism by championing more work by international artists.

When it comes to a permanent collection, however, IMMA has a limited amount of space. The West Wing galleries have traditionally been put aside for displaying works from its collection, but they are not large enough to allow more than a fraction of the museum's thousands of Irish works to be viewed at any one time.

Such limitations notwithstanding, the IMMA has certainly changed in other areas. Where it was once primarily concerned with radical republican art (one thinks not only of Patrick Ireland, but also of Michael Farrell and early Robert Ballagh), recent years have seen retrospectives from the likes of Michael Craig-Martin, whose dizzying, Day-Glo acrylic paintings eschew the political in favour of examining the disjuncture between concepts and objects. (Interestingly, it's a Craig-Martin painting that adorns the cover of the IMMA catalogue, which suggests the museum's concerns are with art for art's sake.)

Meanwhile, Irish female artists like Dorothy Cross – who incorporates found objects, mixed media and sculpture in her work to examine notions of repression, sexuality and man's relationship with the natural world – have enjoyed success as the result of well-received shows here.

All that said, the museum is acutely aware that the strongest gravitational pull for many gallery-goers comes from work by high-profile international artists, so recent years have seen large-scale retrospectives devoted to the likes of Carlos Amorales, Lucian Freud and Howard Hodgkin. So much for parochialism.

DUBLIN BY AREA

This sprawling pub and restaurant hosts live trad music and set dancing every night from 9pm. It can be good fun with the right crowd, but tends to attract large coach tours looking for that Oirish vibe.

Arts & leisure

Cross Gallery

59 Francis Street (473 8978/www. crossgallery.ie). Bus 51B, 78A, 123. **Open** 10am-5.30pm Tue-Fri; 11am-3pm Sat. **Map** p117 F3 **7**
If you happen to be in the Liberties, don't miss the Cross Gallery. The space, reminiscent of galleries on New York's Lower East Side, holds mostly abstract pieces. Its young director has a flair for choosing some of the best emerging Irish painters around. Names to watch out for are Simon English, Siobhan McDonald, Michael Coleman and John Boyd. Recent exhibitions have displayed the works of David King, Clea van der Grijn and Gillian Lawler.

Monster Truck

73 Francis Street (no phone/www. monstertruck.ie). Bus 51B, 78A, 123. **Open** 1-7pm Mon, Tue, Fri-Sun; 6-8pm Thur. No credit cards. **Map** p117 F3 **8**
The gallery arm of a co-operative of largely unknown local artists supported by the Royal Hibernian Academy (p88), Monster Truck exhibits fresh, feisty new work in a variety of media. The turnover is high, with exhibitions set up every Wednesday and preview evenings every Thursday. Names to watch from recent shows are James Kirwan, Magnhild Opdoel, Nina Tanis and Kohei Nekata.

Tivoli

135-138 Francis Street, Kilmainham & Liberties (454 4472). Bus 50, 78A. **Tickets** prices vary. **Map** p117 F2 **9**
This place hosts all manner of live entertainment, from serious drama to musicals. Irish and international shows feature in equal measure, but don't expect to see anything radical.

War Memorial Gardens p119

Malahide Castle p126

Dublin Bay & the Coast

A fair city it may be, but Dublin also has a more outdoorsy side to it, thanks to its natural advantages of sea and mountains. They lend the city beauty whatever the weather, and, on a good day, provide some really stunning views.

The cheapest way to see the coast is still the best: take a DART from one end of the line to the other. Much of the trip is along the constantly changing seashore; the stretch from Sandycove to Bray is gloriously attractive.

Dalkey

There's something absurd in the way inhabitants still refer to this million-euro-a-millimetre area as a 'village'. And yet it's impossible to be cynical when you see this pretty seaside town's charm. Not for nothing have Bono, the Edge, Enya, Lisa Stansfield, Neil Jordan and plenty of hotshot businessmen chosen to buy property here. The influence of Dalkey's wealthy inhabitants can be seen in its many good restaurants, bars and delis.

The real fun here is outdoors. A walk along the main drag – start on Coliemore Road, then on up Sorrento Road and finally Vico Road – gives views of a section of coastline endlessly likened to the Bay of Naples. First is Coliemore Harbour, the launchpad for boats out to Dalkey Island during the summer. Past Coliemore Harbour on the left is Dillon's Park, a grassy space with views out to sea and two

larger-than-life-size goat statues. Next up is Sorrento Terrace, the city's most exclusive address, on a clifftop above the sea.

From Sorrento Terrace, turn on to Vico Road. The rocky Vico bathing spot is where many of the male swimmers from the Forty-Foot seem to have migrated, and it's unashamedly nudist. From here, turn towards the route for Killiney Hill, on top of which stands a wishing stone and Queen Victoria's obelisk. From here you can explore the small forest above Burmah road, or walk down Dalkey Quarry.

Dún Laoghaire

Dún Laoghaire, formerly called Kingstown in honour of the royal visit of George IV, is in the throes of a makeover; the results so far are an excellent blend of old and new. The semi-pedestrianised main street still has its charity shops, greasy spoons and butchers, and the new Pavilion on the seafront covers the upmarket bar, café and restaurant side of things.

The two piers are the focus for much of the area's growing buzz. The more fashionable East Pier is now a weekend destination for half the city; it takes in views of Dún Laoghaire's three members-only yacht clubs and new marina. The less popular West Pier is quite overgrown, but has its loyal fans.

Howth

There never seems to be anyone in Howth but women, children and old people, yet there's a robust feel to the place – and not just because of the bracing wind. Instead of the tinkle of yachts, there's the clunk of trawlers. This is a working village, not a postcard. Beside the DART station is the West Pier, the best place to buy just-caught fish.

Newbridge House & Farm p126

National Transport Museum

Howth Castle Demesne (848 0831/832 0427/www.nationaltransportmuseum. org). Bus 31, 31B/DART Howth. **Open** *June-Aug* 10am-5pm Mon-Fri, 2-5pm Sat, Sun. *Sept-May* 2-5pm Sat, Sun. **Admission** €3.50; €2 reductions; €9 family. No credit cards.

The National Transport Museum is filled with vehicles dating from the 1880s to the 1970s: trams, buses, commercial and military vehicles.

Malahide

This very pretty coastal village has vast green spaces around its castle on one side and ocean on the other; the village has plenty of coffee shops, restaurants and boutiques.

Ardgillen Castle

Balbriggan (849 2212/www.iol.ie/ ~cybmanmc). Bus 33/Balbriggan rail. **Open** *Apr-Sept* 11am-6pm Tue-Sun. *Oct-mid Dec, Feb, Mar* 11am-6pm Wed-Sun. *Mid Dec, Jan* 2-4pm Sun. **Admission** €6.50; €5 reductions; €13 family. No credit cards.

Play away

Your kids will love this.

The capital's newest child-oriented attraction, **Imaginosity** (p127), is a museum that has pretty much everything you're likely to need to get curious young minds fizzing with original ideas. Unsurprisingly, it has proved an instant hit.

It's a fun building, from the 'reflecting pool' that runs beneath it to the colourful mosaics on its roof. There's a theatre space for junior dramatists, a 'climber' that spans two floors of scrambling and clambering opportunities, and a 'construction company' that offers kids the chance to get tooled up with plastic gear and hard hats and set about building, well, something.

Really young children can roll up their sleeves at a dedicated area where all manner of activities encourage them to use and develop their motor skills, senses and language. Elsewhere, there's a village market built to a child's scale, complete with miniature fruit and veg stalls, miniature shopping trolleys and all – and as if that didn't provide role-playing opportunities enough, there's also a scaled-down post office and restaurant.

In other words, if you've come with the kids, you absolutely have to bring them here. And, needless to say, everything from the food in the first-floor café to the layout of the loos has been devised with them in mind. Booking Imaginosity is absolutely essential if you want to come at the weekend.

This romantic 18th-century country house stands in rolling pasture and gardens. There are regular tours; of particular interest is the library, with its secret door behind fake bookshelves.

Malahide Castle

Malahide Castle Demesne, Malahide (846 2184/www.malahidecastle.com). Bus 42/DART Malahide. **Open** *Apr-Oct* 10am-5pm Mon-Sat; 10am-6pm Sun. *Nov-Mar* 10am-5pm Mon-Sat; 11am-5pm Sun. **Admission** *Castle* €7.50; €4.70-€6.30 reductions; €22 family. *Botanic gardens* €4.50.

Historic home of the de Talbots, the castle is an interesting hotchpotch of Norman and Gothic. There's a fine collection of Irish portrait paintings, a café that serves really good, fresh, own-made food, a model railway (summer months only, except Wednesdays), an excellent adventure playground, and the tranquil Talbot Botanic Gardens.

Newbridge House & Traditional Farm

Newbridge Demesne, Donabate (843 6534). Bus 33B/Donabate rail. **Open** *Apr-Sept* 10am-5pm Tue-Sat; 2-6pm Sun. *Oct-Mar* 2-5pm Sat, Sun. **Admission** *House* €7; €3.50-€6 reductions; €18 family. *Farm* €3.80; €2.50-€2.80 reductions; €10 family.

This small Georgian house is modest on the outside, rather grand inside. The Red Drawing Room and Museum of Curiosities are especially interesting – the latter full of stuffed birds, huge shells, a tiny shoe worn by a Chinese woman and a 'scold's bridle'. You can also visit the traditional farmyard, forge, pigturesque pig sties and stables.

Skerries Mill Complex

Skerries (849 5208). Bus 33/Skerries rail. **Open** *Apr-Sept* 10.30am-5.30pm daily. *Oct-Mar* 10.30am-4.30pm daily. **Admission** €6.50; €3.50-€5 reductions; €13 family.

Built in the 1500s, the complex has since been restored, and now includes two large, working five-sail mills and one smaller four-sail watermill. There's a coffee shop and a working bakery.

Sandycove

From Dún Laoghaire's East Pier, stroll along the seafront to Sandycove Green. A new path takes you past Sandycove beach – popular with the bucket-and-spade brigade – all the way to the Forty-Foot, a year-round bathing spot once known for being nudist men-only. It was named after the Fortieth Foot regiment, who were quartered during the 19th century in the adjacent Martello tower.

James Joyce Museum

Joyce Tower, Sandycove (280 9265). Bus 59/DART Sandycove. **Open** *Apr-Sept* 10am-1pm, 2-5pm Mon-Sat; 2-6pm Sun. **Admission** €7.50; €4.70-€6.30 reductions; €22 family.

Famously the setting for the opening chapter of *Ulysses*, in which Joyce mocks Oliver St John Gogarty as 'stately, plump Buck Mulligan', this Martello tower has been restored to match Joyce's description of it. Exhibits are a collection of memorabilia – walking stick, cigar case, guitar, death mask, letters. Best of all is an edition of *Ulysses*, beautifully illustrated with line drawings by Matisse.

Sandymount

There are plenty of beaches to visit, though not all are for swimming. No one would dip in the flat grey waters of Sandymount Strand, but if you fancy a walk in the blustery sea air, this is a good and popular spot. Hardy walkers do the full Poolbeg Peninsula route, taking in the Irishtown Nature Reserve, Sandymount Strand and the South Wall breakwater.

Imaginosity

NEW *The Plaza, Beacon South Quarter, Dublin 18 (217 6130/www. imaginosity.ie). Bus 46B, 11A, 75, 114/Luas Stillorgan.* **Open** 1-5.30pm Mon; 9.30am-5.30pm Tue-Fri; 10am-6pm Sat, Sun. **Admission** €8 adults; €2-€7 reductions. See box p126.

Seapoint

Seapoint is perfect for swimming when the tide is high and laps over the two wide staircases, but the water is too shallow at low tide. On sunny days, the place is packed, mainly with families and children.

Imaginosity

DUBLIN BY AREA

Kilkenny Castle

Worth the Trip

DUBLIN BY AREA

The green hills around Dublin have a wealth of outstanding scenery, prehistoric sites and delightful country accommodation: the beautiful countryside alone is reason enough to spend some time outside the city.

The best way to see the rural sights is by car. You can get to the major towns by train or bus, but then you don't get to see so much landscape or the quaint villages. The following destinations, however, are all well served by public transport or tour buses; enquire at the tourist office (p156).

Kilkenny

Compact and picturesque, with cobbled streets and a singular medieval atmosphere, Kilkenny is a busy, pleasant town filled with good pubs and restaurants. It's also a major crafts centre and the site of summer festivals, most notably Kilkenny Country Roots in May, and the Arts Festival in August.

The town's main draw is obvious as soon as you arrive: the imposing granite edifice of Kilkenny Castle. It's usually besieged by tour buses, but don't be scared away by the crowds: it's well worth a visit and, if you stay long enough to get hungry, the restaurant is excellent.

Elsewhere in Kilkenny, the charming Tholsel ('toll stall') on Main Street is an 18th-century council chamber still used as an office; on Parliament Street is the sturdy Elizabethan Rothe House; and much of the rest of the town seems lifted from a history book.

2-5pm Sun. **Admission** *House* €5; €3-€4 reductions; €10 family. *Garden* free.
Rothe House has been nicely restored, and is now a museum displaying period costumes and various artefacts; not terribly interesting, but the old building is gorgeous and merits a visit on its own. The restored medieval garden opened in April 2008.

St Canice's Cathedral
Irishtown (056 776 4971/www.kilkenny tourism.ie). **Open** *Apr, May, Sept* 10am-1pm, 2-5pm Mon-Sat; 2-5pm Sun. *June-Aug* 9am-6pm Mon-Sat; 2-6pm Sun. *Oct-Mar* 10am-1pm, 2-4pm Mon-Sat; 2-4pm Sun. **Admission** €4; €3 reductions.
Like the castle, the large, medieval St Canice's has had many changes, but enough has been retained for it to rate as a fine example of early Gothic architecture. The adjoining tower offers tremendous views.

Newgrange & Knowth

The ancient site at Newgrange is at once mythological and real: it's one of the most important Stone Age sites in Europe, and also, in Irish lore, the home of the Tuatha de Danainn, cave-dwelling worshippers of the goddess Danu. The deep cavern is covered in strange, geometric patterns, and the meanings of the mysterious zigzags, ovals and crazy spirals have never been fully explained.

What is known for certain is that the ancient passage mounds were built 5,000 years ago, when most tools were made of bone, flint and metal, and then not discovered again until 1699. But how and why the members of a small farming community moved rocks weighing 50 tons over huge distances through inhospitable terrain remains a mystery.

For many, the most interesting part of Newgrange is the tomb's passageway, which descends 19

Even the tourist office on Rose Inn Street is of note: it's one of the few Tudor almshouses in Ireland.

Kilkenny Castle
The Parade (056 770 4100/www. kilkennytourism.ie). **Open** Guided tour only *Apr-May* 10.30am-5pm daily. *June-Aug* 9.30am-7pm daily. *Sept* 10am-6.30pm daily. *Oct-Mar* 10.30am-12.45pm, 2-5 pm daily. **Admission** €5.30; €2.10-€3.70 reductions; €11.50 family.
The existing outer walls date from 1192, but the rest of the building has been rebuilt, restored and renovated. The most recent work was completed in 2001, and made the building more impressive than ever. The grounds are a pretty, well-manicured park leading to artists' and potters' studios.

Rothe House
Parliament Street (056 772 2893/www. rothehouse.com). **Open** (last admission 4.15pm) *Apr-Oct* 10.30am-5pm Mon-Sat; 3-5pm Sun. *Nov-Mar* 10.30am-4.30pm Mon-Sat. *Garden* 10.30am-4.30pm Mon-Thur, 10.30am-4pm Fri;

DUBLIN BY AREA

Newgrange

metres (62 feet); the only time light reaches its depths is on the shortest day of the year. The cavern was designed to line up with the rising sun on 21 December, when a ray of light sweeps down and strikes the back chamber, where it's believed the ashes of the dead were once kept.

You can learn more about it all at the helpful Brú na Bóinne Visitor Centre near the town of Donore. The centre also covers the ancient site of Knowth. Like Newgrange, Knowth is a passage mound decorated with spirals, triangles, concentric circles and other stone carvings. Most unusually, though, Knowth has two passage graves, and its central mound has two chambers – one pointing east and the other west; the eastern passage is an impressive 40 metres (130 feet) long. Like Newgrange, Knowth was designed with the sun in mind, but here light shines on the centre chamber during the spring and autumnal equinoxes.

Although Newgrange and Knowth are generally referred to as 'passage tombs', and both undoubtedly functioned as burial places, archaeologists think there may have been much more to them than that; they're just not sure what. They may have been temples or astronomical observatories.

The passage graves are near the Boyne Valley, where the Battle of the Boyne took place in 1690. In 1688 the Catholic King James II was deposed in favour of his Protestant daughter Mary. In a bid to regain his throne, James fought William of Orange's army at Oldbridge, but his troops were routed, and he had to flee to France. This is where you will find Slane Castle, whose grounds were landscaped by famed British gardener 'Capability' Brown. On the Hill of Slane, outside the town of Slane itself, St Patrick lit an Easter bonfire in 433 as a challenge to the authority of the Kings of Tara. A statue of Patrick marks the spot today.

The other side of that story can be seen on the Hill of Tara, once the seat of the High Kings of Ireland. Tara is the spiritual capital of ancient Ireland and the fount of much folklore. Entrance to the site is free, and there's a visitors' centre inside the church at the top of the hill where you can learn more about the ancient rulers.

Near the Hill of Tara, the town of Trim is well worth a visit. Best among its many sights is Trim Castle, an impressive Anglo-Norman castle. Hugh de Lacy began work on its construction in 1172; when completed, the castle's 20-sided tower had walls three metres (11 feet) thick. It was built to be impregnable – three storeys high, protected by a ditch, a curtain wall and a moat – but the English nevertheless managed to get in (twice) during the English civil war. It was abandoned after Cromwell and his cronies departed. If you think the castle looks familiar, that might be because you've seen *Braveheart*, in which it was used as a stand-in for York.

If you feel up to a walk from here, you can follow the Dublin road from Trim Castle, crossing the river to the ruins of St Patrick's Church (follow the signs). This lovely medieval ruin has well-preserved gravestones, including a 16th-century tomb known locally as the 'jealous couple' – this comes from the fact that the effigies on the tomb lie with a sword carved in between them. Get maps and local information from the handy local visitor centre on Castle Street.

About 20 kilometres (12 miles) north of Trim (or 12 miles west of Newgrange), in the north-west of the county on the N52, is the market town of Kells. This community was first established as a religious settlement in 550, and is most famed for its Book of Kells. The book is now kept in Trinity College (p50), which reduces the town's power of tourist attraction somewhat, although there are some fine Celtic crosses here as well as a Round Tower. There's also the lovely old Church of St Columba in the town centre, which is most notable for standing where the monastic settlement that first received the Book once stood.

Hill of Tara

Brú na Bóinne Visitor Centre

Donore (041 988 0300/www.heritage ireland.ie). **Open** *Nov-Feb* 9.30am-5pm daily. *Mar, Apr, Oct* 9.30am-5.30pm daily. *May-mid June* 9am-6.30pm daily. *Mid June-mid Sept* 9am-7pm daily. **Admission** *Centre* €2.90; €1.60-€2.10 reductions; €7.40 family. *Centre & Newgrange* €5.80; €2.90-€4.50 reductions; €14.50 family. *Centre, Newgrange & Knowth* €10.30; €4.50 children. *Centre & Knowth* €4.50; €1.60-€2.90 reductions.

Access to Newgrange and Knowth is now handled by this visitor centre from where you are shuttled to the sites. In summer this can lead to very long waits. Some swear that if you show up early, you can dodge the masses; we're not so sure, but if you show up late, you might not see anything at all. Since you may have to wait for ages, it's a good thing the centre has a museum, useful videos, models and decent grub.

Wicklow Mountains

The green and hilly countryside of Wicklow starts just a dozen or so miles south of central Dublin, making it one of the easiest and quickest day trips from the city. There's plenty to do there; just remember to take good walking shoes and waterproofs.

Wicklow Town itself is agreeably bustling, with narrow, steep streets climbing up from a pebble beach and fine harbour. If you fancy some exercise, take a walk up the splendid three-kilometre (two-mile) coastal trail that runs from Wicklow Town's seafront past the gaol to Wicklow Head, where it takes in the granite lighthouse at the end. Incidentally, you can also spend the night at the solid old lighthouse, an Irish Landmark Trust property.

Wicklow Gaol

Wicklow Town, Co Wicklow (040 461 599/www.wicklowshistoricgaol.com). **Open** *Mar-Oct* 10am-6pm daily. **Admission** €7.30; €4.50-€6 reductions; €19 families.

The gaol was built in 1702, and held many participants in the 1798 Rising. It's an impressive, literate attraction, and you'll emerge knowing a lot about the gruesome conditions of prison life in the 18th and 19th centuries.

Glendalough and Upper Lake

Essentials

Buswells Hotel p137

Hotels

The last few years have brought some ambitious hotel projects to Dublin. The oh-so-trendy **Dylan** (p141) is one, and the Docklands, in particular, will get several more, as architects like Manuel Aires Mateus inject some glamour into the quays area (p110). Plans are being drafted for a 'monastic' hotel by Grafton Architects, in which polished concrete rooms will give budget accommodation a Le Corbusier spin.

Dublin also has its fair share of duds. There are plenty of dank, dark, hideous establishments, last decorated in 1981 with plaid curtains and floral carpets, and they all seem to charge €100 a night or more. But fear not: in the following pages, we've weeded out the worst and lined up the best each area has to offer.

Information & prices

Rates listed are given as guidelines only: you should check with the hotel to see if prices have changed before you book; hotels change rates frequently. Rates can also vary depending on the day of the week, the month of the year or any special events happening in the city.

Almost all of Dublin's hotels are now no-smoking throughout, so unless otherwise stated, assume this to be the case. Also, it's wise to check hotel websites for special offers, and always ask if any are available before you book. Many hotels will give lower rates for children if you book in advance. VAT is included, but be aware that at the upper end of the market, hotels may also add a 12 to 15 per cent service charge.

ESSENTIALS

Around Trinity College

Trinity Capital Hotel

Pearse Street, Dublin 2 (648 1000/ www.capital-hotels.com). All cross-city buses/DART Pearse. €€€.

Tucked beside Dublin's fire station, the Capital draws business and leisure travellers in equal numbers. The bright rooms are enhanced by subtle art deco touches, but they're a bit small; the decor makes some look like classy dorm rooms, and some of the bathrooms are tiny. Still, service is friendly, and there's a handy restaurant.

Trinity College

College Green, Dublin 2 (896 1177/ www.tcd.ie). All cross-city buses/ DART Pearse. €.

From mid June to early September, Trinity College opens its halls of residence to budget travellers. The 16th-century university is very central, and there are the bonuses of stone buildings, cobbled squares and lots of trees. Choose from single, twin or double rooms, or apartments (in Goldsmith Hall, right next door to the campus); not all the rooms are en suite, so make sure you specify what you're after.

Westin

Westmoreland Street, Dublin 2 (645 1000/www.thewestindublin.com). All cross-city buses. €€€€.

The Westin's imposing 19th-century façade announces an interior of traditional grandeur and exclusivity. The elegant reception area is all marble columns and exquisite plasterwork; a hall of mirrors lines the Westmoreland Street entrance. Rooms are decorated in mahogany and neutral shades, with comfortable beds, soft linen and modern dataports; many have sweeping views of the city. Well worth a splurge.

Around Temple Bar

Abigail's Hostel

NEW *7-9 Aston Quay, Dublin 2 (677 9300/www.abigailshostel.com).* €. See box p138.

SHORTLIST

ESSENTIALS

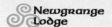

Newgrange Lodge

Formerly an old farmhouse, **Newgrange Lodge** provides a unique venue that offers hotel accommodation and traditional Irish hospitality at bed and breakfast rates to both groups and the independent traveler alike. Located opposite the world famous UNESCO Heritage site of Newgrange, a tomb predating the Pyramids and Stonehenge by 400 years.

- 27 en-suite rooms
- 2 Recreational Areas
- Meeting/conference room
- Communal Kitchen
- Dining Area
- Central Courtyard
  & BBQ Facilities
- Outdoor Terrace Area
- Internet Access Point
- Free Car & Coach Parking

Newgrange Lodge, Donore, Co. Meath, Ireland   Tel: +353 41 988 2478 Fax: +353 41 988 2479
Email: info@newgrangelodge.com   Website: www.newgrangelodge.com

Avalon House

55 Aungier Street, Dublin 2 (475 0001/
www.avalon-house.ie). Bus 16, 16A, 19,
22, 155. €.
See box p138.

Buswells Hotel

23-27 Molesworth Street, Dublin 2
(614 6500/www.quinnhotels.com).
Bus 10, 11, 13, 46A/Luas St Stephen's
Green/DART Pearse. €€€.
This traditional hotel is saved from
feeling stuffy by a strong sense of
class. The rooms in three Georgian
buildings exude charm, from hefty
windows to views of the broad streets
below. Occupying separate buildings
gives the hotel a slightly eccentric feel;
finding your room could be tricky after
a night on the whiskey. But it's undeniably elegant, the rooms are big and
superbly decorated, and the place as a
whole has a marvellous quirky spirit.

Central Hotel

1-5 Exchequer Street, Dublin 2 (679
7302/www.centralhotel.ie). Bus 16,
16A. €€.
This comfortable, 187-year-old hotel is
a prime piece of real estate (right off
Dame Street near Temple Bar) that the
designers haven't yet got their hands
on: floral fabrics and busy carpet patterns everywhere, furniture likely to
have battered edges – and a real sense
of independence. The spacious rooms
and the bathrooms are a bit tired, but
there are lovely architectural touches
and big, old sash windows. The cosy
Library Bar is a haven of civility with
its leather armchairs, blazing fires,
wood panelling and books: it's the
thinking Dubliner's trendy retreat.

Clarence

6-8 Wellington Quay, Dublin 2 (407
0800/www.theclarence.ie). All cross-city
buses/Luas Jervis. €€€€.
Be quick: the building that has housed
the U2 frontmen's hip hotel for 12 years
is slated for demolition – but until then,
it will be business as usual. The large,
soundproofed guest rooms are elegant
and luxuriously appointed; and if you
can tear yourself away from the views

of the Liffey from the big windows in
your room, the Tea Room restaurant
and the Octagon Bar downstairs are
well worth your time and money.
There's also a spa.

Eliza Lodge

23-24 Wellington Quay, Dublin 2 (671
8044/www.dublinlodge.com). All cross-
city buses/Luas Jervis. €€.
Don't be put off by the poky little reception area at this otherwise decent riverside hotel. Some people may be
disturbed by the clatter and rumble of
trucks down on the quays, but double
glazing keeps it in the background, and
the sweeping views of the Liffey more
than make up for the pesky traffic.
Although the rooms won't feature on
any television interior design programme, they're big and bright, and
the price is good for what you get.

Fitzwilliam

St Stephen's Green West, Dublin 2
(478 7000/www.fitzwilliamhotel.com).
All cross-city buses/Luas St Stephen's
Green. €€€€.
A very smart hotel on St Stephen's
Green (with its own Michelin-starred
restaurant, Thornton's; p67), the
Fitzwilliam is undeniably posh – and
yet remains refreshingly free of snob-
bery. That's not to say it doesn't have
plenty to show off: effortlessly elegant
rooms with all the trimmings, right
down to fresh flowers, and bathrooms
packed with lovely products and thick,
fluffy towels. And if food is your thing,
Kevin Thornton's eponymous restaurant will blow your socks off; or there's
the more low-key Citron, beloved of
well-manicured ladies.

Four Courts

15-17 Merchants Quay, Dublin 8 (672
5839/www.fourcourtshostel.com). All
cross city buses/Luas Four Courts. €.
Set in several pretty Georgian buildings overlooking the Liffey, this friendly hostel has all the basics, and a few
bonuses besides. Its site at the river's
edge is lovely, and the rooms have big
windows, wood floors, desks and other
touches that make the metal bunk beds

Cheap 'n' classy

Designer dens on a budget.

Abigail's

For such an overpriced city, Dublin has some surprisingly affordable design-conscious accommodation, and three addresses in particular are leading the crusade to provide budget sleeps with a generous dash of style.

The newest kid on the budget block is **Abigail's Hostel** (p135) in Temple Bar, and it has a refreshingly sunny approach to shoestring accommodation. You may find yourself wedged into a room with seven other people, but the decor is modern and welcoming, and the common areas smartly decked out. Shared guest rooms vary in size from two to eight bunks, but there are a couple of single rooms for a few euros more. The place never gets rowdy, and security is reassuringly tight. Prices start at a recession-resistant €10 a night.

Another hit among budget travellers is **Avalon House** (p137), a pleasantly warm and cheery guesthouse in a lovely old red brick building just a few minutes

from St Stephen's Green. Its pine floors, high ceilings and open fireplace give it a homely feel, and rooms range from dorms to doubles. Its most recent addition is an outpost of the excellent Bald Barista café up the road (p59), perfect for charging the system with a morning espresso and planning the day. Dorm beds start at €14, single rooms up to €36.

But if sharing a bedroom with five strangers isn't your idea of fun, and you plan to stay in Dublin for a week or more, check out the home comforts of **Solar House** (p146). The solar-heated eco-hotel in the suburbs is divided into four double self-catering apartments, equipped with breakfast bar, TV, hairdryer and so on. Since it opened 11 years ago, word of mouth has spread, and students and travellers come from as far away as China and Australia to stay for as long as a year at a time. Prices start at €385 per week for two people sharing.

more bearable. It has 24-hour access, free continental breakfast, laundry, a games room, internet access, good security, and a car park: more than most hostels give you for the money.

Kinlay House

2-12 Lord Edward Street, Dublin 2 (679 6644/www.kinlaydublin.ie). All cross-city buses. €.

This beautiful red brick building in one of Dublin's oldest neighbourhoods (just steps from Christ Church Cathedral; p58) is a great setting for a hostel. It's quiet enough for a good night's kip, but close enough to Temple Bar to be within post-pub crawl stumbling distance. There's a large self-catering kitchen and dining room, a TV room and meeting room. Dorms are small but clean, and the front desk is open non-stop.

Morgan

10 Fleet Street, Dublin 2 (679 3939/ www.themorgan.com). All cross-city buses. €€€.

Designed to within an inch of its life, the Morgan is, above all, trendy; but it's also a very comfortable and attractive spot in which to lay your head. The spacious bedrooms are decked out in calming pale tones, and the cocktail bar has tapas, a DJ and occasional bongo player. Rooms looking out on to Fleet Street can be noisy in the small hours; ask for a room at the back of the hotel or on one of the upper floors. It also has apartments for extended stays.

Paramount

Parliament Street & Essex Street, Dublin 2 (417 9900/www.paramount hotel.ie). All cross-city buses. €€€.

You'd never guess it from sitting in the Turk's Head on a Saturday night, but this hotel is a hidden gem. It's not peaceful – the aforementioned bar packs in party people most nights – but it looks quite good. The rooms are reminiscent of 1930s chic, done up in subtle tobacco tones, with leather headboards, dark wood furnishings and soft lighting. Ask for one on the upper floors if you don't have earplugs.

Temple Bar Hotel

15-17 Fleet Street, Dublin 2 (677 3333/www.towerhotel group.ie). All cross-city buses/ Luas Abbey Street. €€.

Temple Bar has a raucous rep (the stag parties, the vomit on pavements), and it has to be said that this hugely popular hotel is right in the thick of the action. But if that doesn't put you off, there's much to be said for staying right in the centre of things – and, despite its busy nightclub, the hotel does well to maintain an air of civility. There's a grown-up reception area, comfortable (albeit plain) rooms, and a team of helpful, switched-on staff. Even so, if you're looking for peace and quiet, this probably isn't the place for you.

Trinity Lodge

12 South Frederick Street, Dublin 2 (617 0900/www.trinitylodge.com). All cross-city buses/Luas St Stephen's Green. €€.

Set in a nicely maintained Georgian property, Trinity Lodge has a chic, laid-back style. There's a pleasant restaurant where you can expect high-quality nosh of a morning (own-baked bread, freshly squeezed orange juice and the like); in a second building across the road, six more rooms have a more contemporary feel but are equally well done. Staff are friendly, and the place is well located for the restaurants and bars of the city centre. Because the building is listed, there's no lift.

Westbury Hotel

Grafton Street, Dublin 2 (679 1122/ www.jurys doyle.com). All cross-city buses/Luas St Stephen's Green. €€€€.

After a €14 million refurbishment in 2008, this upmarket hotel is looking very swanky indeed. The understated style of its guest rooms exudes wealth and sophistication, and its bright, spacious lobby is a discreetly grand place for a drink (in the high-rolling bar or the café overlooking Grafton Street). Its central site makes the Westbury a fine base for weekenders who want a hassle-free HQ for sights and shops.

ESSENTIALS

KILRONAN HOUSE

⚜ GRADE A GUESTHOUSE ⚜

Perfectly positioned just around the corner from St Stephen's Green and within walking distance to Grafton Street, Trinity College, Dublin Castle and much more, beautiful **Kilronan House** offers the perfect escape from the hustle and bustle of vibrant Dublin.

Built in 1834, the height of the Georgian era, Kilronan House's 12 well appointed rooms are the ideal haven for singles, couples and families wanting to enjoy the sights of Dublin.

Operating as a successful guesthouse for over 60 years, **Kilronan House** has managed to retain the perfect blend of old fashioned Irish hospitality and Georgian charm. Our guests are provided with warm, attentive and personal service – the key to remaining a long standing favourite in the Dublin area.

Internet (wireless). No-smoking rooms. Parking (free). TV.

Kilronan House, 70 Adelaide Road, Dublin 2.
Tel. 475 5266 Fax 478 2841 www.kilronanhouse.com
Air Coach from Dublin Airport. Rooms 12.
Rates €55.00 - €200.00 single/double/triple (including Full Breakfast).
Credit AmEx, DC, MC, Maestro, Laser.

Welcome to Kilronan House..... a place to call home

Around St Stephen's Green

Conrad Hotel

Earlsfort Terrace, Dublin 2 (602 8900/ www.conradhotels.com). Bus 10, 11, 13, 14, 15, 44, 46A, 47, 48, 86/Luas St Stephen's Green. €€€€.

The long-established Conrad is a firm favourite among the suited, laptop-wielding types who have made Dublin the business hub that it is: there are fast internet connections and big desks. Bedrooms are nicely done in neutral colours, with big windows, individual temperature controls for the air con, and fabulous bathrooms. The hotel pub might lack character, but local office workers still fill it every night; and the Alex restaurant is a particularly sleek hotel diner for people with expense accounts.

Dylan

NEW *Eastmoreland Place, Dublin 4 (660 3000/www.dylan.ie). Bus 11,13, 16, 16A/Luas Charlemont.* €€€€.

Cool enough to stay in the Dylan? You wish. This is the boutique hotel everyone's talking about: from the oversized lanterns strewn around its entrance to the iPods in its immaculate guest rooms, every detail of this hotel has been carefully thought out. There's a swish lobby, stylish cocktail bar, sumptuously upholstered furniture, yards of trendy wallpaper and a bright, white, minimalist terrace. Guest rooms are a triumph of understatement with flashes of boldness (the bedheads, in particular, are stunning). This is serious luxury for people who expect nothing less.

Harrington Hall

69-70 Harcourt Street, Dublin 2 (475 3497/www.harringtonhall.com). Bus 10, 11, 15A, 15B, 16, 16A, 20B, 62/Luas Harcourt. €€€.

This lovely hotel occupies a property that was once the home of Timothy Charles Harrington, former Lord Mayor of Dublin, who clearly had excellent architectural taste. The exquisite stuccoed ceilings have been

Kilronan House p142

kept, and there's much else to praise: the warmth, attentiveness and personal touch of the service, the beautifully appointed lobby and the spotless, simple but elegant bedrooms. This is one of Dublin's outstanding small hotels.

Hilton Dublin

Charlemont Place, Grand Canal, Dublin 2 (402 9988/www.hilton.co.uk/dublin). Bus 14, 15, 44, 48A/Luas Charlemont. €€€.

The main selling point of this modern chain hotel is its tranquil setting overlooking the banks of the Grand Canal, offering a view so bucolic you could forget you're in the middle of the city. The bedrooms are decorated in contemporary style, and they get lots of light. In honour of its core clientele, the Hilton has a full complement of business facilities. The restaurant overlooks the canal, which makes up a bit for the hotel's rather uninspiring interior.

Kilronan House

70 Adelaide Road, Dublin 2 (475 5266/ www.kilronanhouse.com). Bus 11,13, 16, 16A/Luas Harcourt. €€.

It may look like just another B&B from its modest terraced façade but Kilronan House is an elegant and, above all, welcoming place that has been renovated with real class. The staff are never short on enthusiasm, and the massive, varied breakfasts served in the sunny front room will set you up for the day. Some of the guest rooms in the handsome Victorian building still have original period features and high ceilings; newer bedrooms don't, although they do have a little more space.

Merrion Hotel

Upper Merrion Street, Dublin 2 (603 0600/www.merrionhotel.com). Bus 10, 13, 13A/DART Pearse. €€€€.

Set in four restored, listed Georgian houses, the Merrion doesn't shy away from a little frill here, a delicate striped couch there. The public spaces are dominated by quiet drawing rooms where fires glow in hearths, and the impressive contemporary art on the walls is part of one of the country's largest private collections. Service is discreetly omnipresent, and the spacious rooms

overlook the government buildings or the hotel's 18th-century-inspired gardens of acacia and lilac. Relax in the Tethra Spa, and dine at the Michelin-starred Patrick Guilbaud restaurant (p84) or at the cheaper and more atmospheric Cellar (p80).

Number 31

31 Leeson Close, Dublin 2 (676 5011/ www.number31.ie). Bus 10, 46A/Luas Charlemont. €€.

This unique guesthouse, in one of the city's most fashionable locales, is a real find, combining modern design with an almost rural tranquillity. Most of the soothingly decorated bedrooms occupy a Georgian townhouse; a few are in the beautifully designed modern mews building where delicious own-made breakfasts are served. Warm yourself in front of the peat fire in the sunken lounge, or wander through the lush gardens for some green therapy.

Shelbourne Hotel

27 St Stephen's Green North, Dublin 2 (663 4500/www.marriott.co.uk). Bus, 11, 14, 15. €€€€.

Merrion

Having had more than €40 million lavished on it by the Marriott empire, the Shelbourne is looking good. It always was the doyenne of Dublin hotels (albeit in a slightly faded kind of way), and now this five-star is a major contender again. From the candelabras in its marble lobby to the Egyptian cotton sheets and sumptuous bathrooms, the Shelbourne is all about good living. The Horseshoe Bar is a great nook for a nightcap, and the Lord Mayor's is the place for afternoon teas.

Around O'Connell Street

Abode Apartments

Quay Apartments, Eden Quay, Dublin 1 (814 7000/www.abodedublin.com). All cross-city buses/Luas Abbey Street. €€.

One in a string of locations around the city, this smart riverside apartment address is a nice alternative to a hotel. Floor-to-ceiling windows let in plenty of daylight, and make the most of the views; the video intercom provides the peace of mind that is sometimes missing in Dublin's self-catering sector. Kitchens are perfectly serviceable, and the staff (who can be contacted 24/7) are helpful and pleasant. Other locations include the very central Adelaide Square, and Temple Bar's award-winning Wooden Building.

Cassidy's Hotel

Cavendish Row, Upper O'Connell Street, Dublin 1 (878 0555/www. cassidyshotel.com). All cross-city buses/Luas Abbey Street. €€€.

The family-owned Cassidy's Hotel is across the street from the historic Gate Theatre, and within about ten minutes' walk of Temple Bar and Dame Street's hustle. The hotel is larger than it looks from the outside (there are more than 100 bedrooms in there, somehow), and has a handy restaurant and a cosy bar. Rooms are smallish and simple, but not cramped or uncomfortable. Rooms at the back are quieter, but those at the

ESSENTIALS

Number 31 p143

With an interior by John Rocha and every fancy boutique touch – from in-room iPod docks or Macs with wireless keyboards to gorgeous bathrooms with aromatherapy toiletries and sunken baths – the Morrison lives up to its name for sophisticated luxury. A lot of work has been done on the interior in recent years, and the results are stunning. The rooms have Egyptian cotton bed linen and Portuguese limestone in the bathrooms; and the two bars (especially the cosy Morrison Bar; p106) and the Halo restaurant are design-literate, well-run operations.

Mount Eccles Court

42 North Great Georges Street, Dublin 1 (873 0826/www.eccleshostel.com) All cross-city buses/Luas Abbey Street. €.
This lovely little hostel in a Georgian building is a great option for those who find bigger facilities intimidating. Its ten bedrooms and ten dorms are secured with keycard locks and are neatly decorated with neutral walls and nice touches like potted plants. There's 24-hour access, bedding (including sheets), luggage lockers, internet access, bike storage, hot showers, and TV and music lounges. It also has apartments for rent.

front have a better view. Charmingly, if you've forgotten to bring a good book, the front desk will lend you one.

Gresham Hotel

23 Upper O'Connell Street, Dublin 1 (874 6881/www.gresham-hotels.com). Bus 11, 13/Luas Abbey Street. €€€€.
A key part of Dublin's political and leisure history (it featured in the Easter Rising as a refuge), the Gresham has been taking care of visitors for 200 years. The grand façade, vast lobby and charming bar are all elegant, but not overwhelmingly so; here it's all about comfort. A lengthy renovation has given this grande dame a badly needed upgrade, and all rooms now have luxurious fabrics in soothing tones and all the usual four-star extras.

Morrison

Ormond Quay, Dublin 1 (887 2400/ www.morrisonhotel.ie). Bus 30, 90/ Luas Jervis. €€€€.

North Quays & Docklands

Clarion Dublin IFSC

International Financial Services Centre, Dublin 1 (433 8800/www.clarion hotelifsc.com). All cross-city buses/ DART Connolly. €€€.
Yes, it's a chain hotel, and big with business travellers; but don't be put off. This is an excellent place: attractive, well run, fabulously located, with decent prices and lots of extras. The guest rooms are spacious, with sweeping views of the Liffey; they're done in soothing neutral colours, all cream and taupe; they have Egyptian cotton duvets, large TVs, free broadband and even game consoles. The laid-back atmosphere in the stylish bar and

restaurant is relaxing; there's a fully-equipped gym and a truly gorgeous heated indoor pool. As chain hotels go, it doesn't get much better than this.

Days Inn

95-98 Talbot Street, Dublin 1 (874 9202/www.daysinntalbot.com). Bus 33, 41/Luas Abbey Street. €€.
Someone has been doing some thinking at the Days Inn, with the result that now, where the boring chain hotel decor once was, you'll find lots of brushed wood, chrome and neutral colours. The bedrooms are a bit on the small side, but they're nice enough to rest in between bouts of shopping on nearby O'Connell Street.

Isaac's Hostel

2-5 Frenchman's Lane, Dublin 1 (855 6215/www.isaacs.ie). All cross-city buses/Luas Busáras/DART Connolly. €.
Near Busáras bus depot and Connolly Street train station, this is the aristocrat of Dublin's hostels. Isaac's takes the backpacker concept of humble frugality and turns it on its head. Calling itself 'Dublin's first VIP hostel', it has the usual mix of bunk beds, lockers and TV rooms, but adds a heady cocktail of extras like polished wood floors, a restaurant and an attractive (free) sauna. There's also internet access, a kitchen for guests, pool tables – and a friendly and relaxing atmosphere.

Park Inn

Smithfield Village, Dublin 7 (817 3838/www.park inn.ie). Bus 25, 26, 37, 39, 67, 68, 69, 70/Luas Smithfield. €€.
The Park Inn deserves a mention if only for the fact that it manages to not betray what it is: a chain hotel. In every way, this characterful place is a welcome slice of easy-living modernity among the historic buildings of charming Smithfield Village. Irish music is one of the hotel's themes: suites are named after Irish musicians, and there are large music murals in the bar and CDs on the stereos in most rooms. The bedrooms themselves are modern and bright – perhaps too much so – but the overall feeling is one of comfort.

Shelbourne p143

Dublin Bay & the Coast

Clontarf Castle Hotel

Castle Avenue, Clontarf, Dublin 3 (833 2321/www.clontarfcastle.ie). Bus 130/DART Clontarf Road. €€€€.
Since it had €10 million spent on it, Clontarf Castle is looking every inch the swanky modern hotel (except for the elements of the 12th-century structure that have been artfully integrated into the design). The original castle was built in 1172 by Hugh de Lacy, and what remains (not much) gives the hotel a unique atmosphere. There might be the odd suit of armour or faded tapestry dotted about the place, but it's far from fusty, thanks to striking modern touches like the new glass entrance. Pared-down decor, cast-iron bathtubs and mod cons aplenty ensure the guest rooms are suitably grand.

ESSENTIALS

Deer Park Hotel & Golf Courses

Howth, Co. Dublin (832 2624/www.deerpark-hotel.ie). Bus 31A, 31B/DART Howth. €€.

Unquestionably the best thing about this hyper-modern hotel, perched above the sleepy fishing village of Howth, is its sweeping view of the rugged North Dublin coast. It's enduringly popular with golfers and rugby weekenders, and its location (some distance off the main road) makes it tranquil and relaxing. Rooms are spacious, and most enjoy grand sea vistas; there's a large indoor swimming pool with sauna and steam room, a spa and tennis courts, and the bar has a sizeable outdoor area.

Fitzpatrick Castle Dublin

Killiney, Co. Dublin (230 5400/www.fitzpatrickhotels.com). DART Dalkey. €€€.

Standing nobly at the top of the hill overlooking the village of Dalkey, the Fitzpatrick is a regal-looking place that does indeed look like a castle. In fact, it's a crenellated manor house, but no less impressive for it: guest rooms are decked out in a kind of country chic (some with truly extraordinary sea views), and the rambling old lounge is a joy, filled with lots of sofas, pianos and working fireplaces. The elegant 20-metre indoor swimming pool is handy, and there's a decent basement restaurant and a more expensive formal restaurant for fine dining; the Library bar is lively and attractive with a wine and cocktail menu to please drinkers.

Marina House

7 Dunleary Road, Dún Laoghaire (284 1524/www.marinahouse.com). Bus 7, 46A/DART Monkstown. €.

This popular hostel has dorms as well as one double and one twin room. Amenities include laundry facilities, a TV room and a kitchen open to guests. A cheap and pleasant way to get a little sea air.

Solar House

195 Vernon Avenue, Clontarf, Dublin 3 (833 7589/www.thesolarhouse.com). Bus 130/DART Clontarf Road. €.

See box p138.

Morrison p144

Getting Around

Airports

Dublin Airport is about 13 construction-plagued kilometres (eight slow miles) north of the city, and is managed by **Aer Rianta** (814 1111, www.dublinairport.com). It's small, but packed with shops. The airport also has currency exchange facilities and car rental desks, plus a tourist information office (open from 8am to 10pm daily) that can provide maps and information as well as accommodation booking.

As there's no rail service to Dublin Airport, the only public transport is Dublin Bus, which runs the **Airlink** coach service (873 4222/www.dublinbus.ie). There are two routes: the **747** (5.45am-11.30pm Mon-Sat; 7.15am-11.30pm Sun) runs from the airport to O'Connell Street (in the city centre) and Central Bus Station, and the **748** (6.50am-9.30pm Mon-Sat; 7am-10.05pm Sun) runs to Central Bus Station, Tara Street (DART Station), Aston Quay (in the centre), Wood Quay (by Christ church) and Heuston Rail Station. On the 747 route, buses run every ten minutes Monday to Saturday, and every 20 minutes on Sunday. On the 748 route, buses run every 30 minutes daily. Both journeys take 25 minutes to the centre of town and 40 minutes to Heuston Rail Station; tickets, which can be bought from the driver, are €6/€10 return (€3 for children/€5 return).

The 747 buses run to the airport at 5.15am-10.50pm Monday to Saturday and 7.35am-11.15pm on Sunday; the 748 runs to the airport from 7.15am-10.30pm Monday to Saturday and 7.50am-10.50pm on Sunday.

Two non-express buses, the **16A** and **41**, also serve the airport (€2 single); timetables are displayed at the bus stops outside the airport's Arrivals terminal. Take note: no large items of baggage are allowed on these buses.

To & from the airport

To get into town from the airport, follow signs to the M1, then take it south towards Dublin. When you get to the M50 ring road, either loop around to enter Dublin from whichever side is closest to the part of town you need, or stay on the M1, which becomes the N1 when it enters the city limits. The journey into town takes about 20 minutes, although the frequent construction on the M1 may slow you down, particularly during rush hour.

The big, blue private **Aircoach** service (844 7118/www.aircoach.ie, open 9am-5.30pm Mon-Sat) runs from the terminal to Ballsbridge in the southern suburbs via the city centre (O'Connell Street). A second route runs from the airport to Leopardstown taking in the city, Donnybrook and Stillorgan: its buses run hourly between midnight and 4am; every 20 minutes 4-6am and 8pm-midnight; and every ten minutes 6am-8pm. The trip usually takes 40 minutes, but can take up to an hour at rush hour.

It's marginally more expensive (€7 single, €12 return, €1 5-12s, free under-5s), but makes up for that by being impressively prompt, pleasant and reliable. You can buy tickets just outside the arrivals lounge. Aircoach also sells the **Dublin Pass**, which provides a guide book and entry to over 30 attractions for €31 across the city.

Taxis are plentiful and a journey into the city centre will usually cost around €25-€30.

Arriving by coach

Travelling by coach in Ireland is a good deal cheaper than travelling by rail, though the Irish road network is still not as good as it might be. The largest nationwide coach service is **Bus Éireann** (836 6111, www.buseireann.ie), which operates out of Dublin's Central Bus Station (Busáras). Private bus companies include **Rapid Express** (679 1549, www.jjkavanagh.ie).

Central Bus Station (Busáras)
Store Street (recorded information 836 6111 6am-11pm daily/www.bus eireann.ie). **Open** 9.30am-6pm daily. The information desk here can provide details of local and national bus and coach services, as well as tours, including services to Northern Ireland.

Arriving by ferry

Ferries are still likely to remind you of backpacking trips, but even in these days of cheap trans-channel flights, some people prefer them – if only for the views and the lure of spending time out on the water. While those on driving tours may find that it makes economic sense to take the car along (especially if travelling in a group), it's no longer cheap to cross by boat: two people with a car can expect to pay around £242 return to sail from Liverpool to Dublin in high season. Note that some lines give a 20 per cent discount to members of youth hostel organisations.

Ferries from Dublin sail to Holyhead (North Wales), the Isle of Man, and Liverpool on the UK mainland. There are two ferry ports in and around Dublin: Dublin Port, about three kilometres (two miles) from the centre (on Alexandra Road, 887 6000, www.dublinport.ie, bus 53, 53A to/from the centre), and Dún Laoghaire.

Arriving by train

The national railway network is run by **Iarnród Éireann** (836 6222, www.irishrail.ie). Trains to and from Dublin use **Connolly Station** or **Heuston Station**, both on the city's north side. As a rule of thumb, Connolly serves Belfast, Rosslare and Sligo; Heuston serves Galway, Westport, Tralee, Killarney, Kildare, Cork, Limerick, Ennis and Waterford. The Enterprise service to Belfast is clean, fast and comfortable, but it's not representative; some other InterCity services can be slow, grotty and uncomfortable.

Bikes may be carried on most mainline routes; ask where to store them, as regulations vary with the type of train.

Public transport

Iarnród Éireann runs the **DART** electric rail and suburban rail services, and **Dublin Bus** (Bus Atha Cliath) is responsible for the city buses. Several combined bus and rail tickets are available, so work out where and how much you want to travel and see which type suits best.

There is **left luggage** at Busáras (703 2434/www.buseirann.ie), Connolly Station (703 2358), Heuston Station (703 2132) and Dublin Airport (814 4633). Rates range from €1.50-10 per 24 hours.

Bus

Bus stops look like tall green or blue lollipops. They usually (though not always) display a timetable but rarely have a shelter. 'Set down only' means the bus only lets passengers off there, so don't hang around waiting; look for a bus sign that doesn't bear those three words. Note a Dublin curiosity: you board buses at the front and get off at the front, too: the middle doors seldom open.

More than 150 bus routes criss-cross the city centre, so you'll usually find a bus stop close by. Timetables at bus stops are often defaced, so your best bet is to get up-to-date versions from Dublin Bus's Headquarters (59 Upper O'Connell Street, 873 4222, www.dublinbus.ie). Buses are generally frequent, but most only keep loosely to their schedules, so allow plenty of time – especially in rush hour and during the whole of Friday afternoon.

Fares are set by city zone, or 'stage'. There are more than 23 stages in and around Dublin, and you can check timetables to see what stage your destination is in. Fares are €1.05 for a journey within stages one to three, €1.50 for stages four to seven, €1.70 for stages eight to 13, and up to €4.30 to take a bus from the centre to a far-flung suburban stage.

You can buy tickets or bus passes from tourist offices and newsagents, or you can pay the driver the appropriate fare on boarding the bus in coins only. If you choose to do the latter, exact change is a good idea: drivers can't give change, though they will issue you a ticket for the amount of the overpayment, and you can then have this money returned at Dublin Bus. If you need to buy a ticket, board on the left-hand side of the front entrance; the right-hand side is reserved for passengers who have pre-paid bus passes, which are easier and cheaper.

If you plan to do a lot of travel by bus, it's a good idea to buy one of these passes. Options include a one-day pass (€6), three-day pass (€11.50), five-day pass (€18.50), seven-day pass (€23) and one-day family pass (€10). All offer unlimited use of all Dublin Bus services for their specified period. There's also a range of student offers, for which you need ID and a Travelsave stamp from the Dublin Bus offices.

Night buses

Normal bus services end at around 12.30am, but **Nitelink** buses run every night except Sunday along many different routes from the city centre to the suburbs. Services leave from D'Olier Street, Westmoreland Street and College Street, starting at around 12.30am, then departing every half hour or so until 4.30am. The fare is €5. Check with tourist offices or Dublin Bus for timetables and routes.

Rail services

The **DART** (Dublin Area Rapid Transit, www.irishrail.ie) and **Suburban Rail** lines provide a faster and arguably more pleasant alternative to buses for journeys beyond the city centre. Central DART stations include **Connolly**, **Tara Street**, **Pearse** and **Grand Canal Dock**. Most of the DART runs outside the city centre, serving the north and south suburbs from Greystones and Bray in the south to Howth and Malahide in the north. The DART is supplemented by Suburban Rail routes that range as far as Dundalk in County Louth, Arklow in County Wicklow, Mullingar in County Westmeath and County Kildare.

Rail tickets are available from all DART and Suburban Rail stations,

ESSENTIALS

as well as from the **Rail Travel Centre** (35 Lower Abbey Street, 836 6222, www.irishrail.ie). On buying a single or return rail ticket, specify the final destination so the ticket can be validated for a connecting bus service if that is required.

A new transport option is the **LUAS** tram system (1-800 300 604/www.luas.ie). This state-of-the-art light rail system connects you to the city centre, many of Dublin's top tourist attractions and the best shopping areas. Luas (the word is Irish for 'speed') has two routes. The red line runs from Connolly Rail Station to Tallaght in south-west Dublin. The green line runs from St Stephen's Green in the centre to Sandyford in the southern suburbs. An extension to the red line will be complete by the end of 2009.

Luas operates 5.30am-12.30am Mon-Fri, 6.15am-12.30am Sat and 7am-11.30pm Sun. Single fares start at €1.50; a one day adult pass costs €5. Combined Luas and Dublin Bus tickets cost €6.80. Buy tickets before boarding; there are ticket machines on the platform at every stop.

Taxis

A multitude of taxi companies operate and taxis tend to be plentiful (though finding one on Saturday nights can be tricky). Expect to pay high prices round the clock. There are 24-hour ranks at Abbey Street and Upper O'Connell Street on the northside, and at Aston Quay, College Green and St Stephen's Green (north). Taxis can often be found outside major hotels.

Some private companies offer fixed rates for certain journeys and don't charge a pick-up fee; licensed cabs run on a meter. The minimum charge is €3.80 for the first kilometre or 170 seconds between 8am and 8pm. Between 8pm and 8am Monday to Saturdays and all day on Sundays and public holidays the initial rate is €4.80; each additional kilometre is charged at 95c (8am-8pm) or 34c per minute and €1.25 per kilometre or 44c per minute from 8pm-8am, and all day on Sundays and public holidays. Extra charges of €1 are levied for extra passengers. (One child under 12 travels free; 2 or 3 children will be charged an extra €1.) You'll be charged an extra €2 if you hire a taxi by phone.

If you have any complaints about taxis, contact the **Irish Taxi Drivers' Federation** (836 4166).

Castle Cabs *802 2222*
City Cabs *872 2222*
Co-Op Taxis *676 6666*
Pony Cabs *661 0101/*
www.ponyexpress.ie

Driving

Dublin's roads are truly hellish: traffic jams at rush hour (morning and night) make the daily commute a grind for locals, and driving an ordeal for visitors. Worse still, the street signs in Gaelic and English are too dark and the writing too small for the names of the streets to be easily read in either language – which means it's all too easy to get very lost, very quickly. The system of one-way streets in the centre – often not shown on maps – can get drivers unfamiliar with the city into a flat spin. Then there's construction disruption.

What's more, public transport is quite good in Dublin, so there's even less reason to drive; buses are reliable and frequent, and have a special lane for faster trips; the DART rail system will whisk you out to the coast in a few short minutes.

Most people who spend all of their time in the city don't even bother renting a car. If you bring your own car, or rent one on the spot, drive carefully. And be sure to get out of town. Country roads may not always be of the highest standard, but they're rarely choked with traffic and construction.

European Union, United States and international driving licences are valid in Ireland. Speed limits are 50kph (31mph) in urban areas, 80kph (50mph) in suburban areas, 100kph (62mph) on main roads (excluding urban areas and motorways) and 120kph (75mph) on dual carriageways and on the motorways.

Seatbelts must be worn by drivers and all passengers of cars and light vans. The alcohol limit, as in the UK and most US states, is 80 milligrams per 100 millilitres of blood. Cars drive on the left-hand side of the road.

Breakdown services

There are many garages in Dublin that will help if you have a breakdown. The following places offer 24-hour support.

Automobile Association
617 9999/www.aaireland.com
Glenalbyn Motors *460 4050*
Kane Motors *833 8143*
RAC *1-800 805 498/www.rac.ie*

Parking

Parking spaces in the centre of Dublin are expensive and can be difficult to find. Expect to pay at least €2 per hour in the centre. Computerised billboards throughout the city list availability in the major car parks. All on-street parking in the city centre is pay-to-park: there should be an automatic ticket machine on each street. Be warned: clamping is widely used, even in residential areas.

Vehicle hire

Unless you're a committed (and patient) car driver, there's no point hiring a car for your stay in Dublin. However, if you plan to travel outside the capital, a vehicle is essential, since public transport is far less reliable and infrequent away from the city. You must have a valid driving licence and a credit card in order to hire a car. All the car hire companies listed here also have outlets at Dublin Airport. All advise that you pre-book.

Avis *1-605 7500/airport 605 7500/ www.avis.com*
Budget *837 9611/airport 844 5150/ www.budget.ie*
Hertz *709 3060/airport 844 5466/ www.hertz.com*
National Car Rental *260 3771/ airport 844 4162/www.carhire.ie*

Cycling

The biggest problem with cycling in Dublin is not the air pollution, nor avoiding the mad drivers, but rather finding a safe place to keep your bike: Dublin railings are filled with single wheels dangling from locks. If you have to park outdoors, try to use two locks – a strong one for the frame and back wheel and another for the front wheel – and take your lights, saddle and any other detachables with you.

Cycle hire

For cycle hire you can expect to pay something in the region of €20 per day (based on a 24 hour period), although there are usually weekly rates (€80) and group discounts that will reduce the price somewhat. A refundable deposit of €200 is required. A useful cycle hire operation is **Cycle Ways Bike Rental** (185-186 Parnell Street, 873 4748, www.cycleways.com).

Resources A-Z

Accident & emergency

Dial **999** or **112** for Fire, Garda (police) and ambulances.

Credit card loss

As you would at home, first inform the police and then contact the relevant 24-hour number:

American Express *customer services 1-800 282 728/travellers' cheques 1-800 626 000*
Diners' Club *0818 300 026/ authorisation service 1-800 709 944*
MasterCard *1-800 557 378*
Visa *1-800 558 002*

Customs

If you're entering Ireland from outside the EU, you're entitled to the following duty-free allowances: 200 cigarettes or 100 cigarillos or 50 cigars or 250 grams of tobacco; two litres of port, sherries or fortified wines or 1 litre spirits or strong liqueurs (over 22 per cent alcohol); two litres of table wine; 60 millilitres of perfume; 250 millilitres of toilet water; €184 worth of goods, including gifts and souvenirs.

If you're entering Ireland from inside the EU (excluding new member states), you're entitled to the following duty-free allowances: 800 cigarettes or 400 cigarillos or 200 cigars or one kilogram of tobacco; ten litres of port, sherries or fortified wines or ten litres of spirits or strong liqueurs (over 22 per cent alcohol); 90 litres of table wine; unlimited perfume; unlimited toilet water; €175 worth of goods, including gifts and souvenirs.

Dental emergency

The website of the **Irish Dental Association** (295 0072/www. dentist.ie) provides a quick and easy way to find a registered dentist in your area.

Disabled

More and more places provide facilities for disabled people – call ahead to check.

Dublin Bus has a lot of wheelchair-accessible buses, and more are added all the time. Few railway or **DART** stations were built with wheelchair users in mind, but **Iarnród Éireann** makes an effort to accommodate people who contact them in advance: staff will meet you at the station, accompany you to the train, arrange a parking space and set up ramps. All **Luas** trams have designated spaces for wheelchairs. Wheelchair users should enter through the double doors in the middle of the tram, where information on where and how to position the wheelchair is shown.

For details of access to stations nationwide, call any DART station or train station and ask for the *InterCity Guide for Mobility Impaired Passengers*. For further information, contact the **Department of Transport** (44 Kildare Street, Southside, 670 7444, www.transport.ie).

Electricity

Like the rest of Europe, Ireland uses a 220-240V, 50-cycle AC voltage, with three-pin plugs (as in the UK). Adaptors are widely available at airport shops. Note too that Irish and UK VCRs and televisions use a different frequency from those in the USA.

Embassies & consulates

For embassies and consulates not listed below, consult the Golden Pages. Note that many countries (such as New Zealand) do not maintain a full embassy in Dublin. In those cases the embassy in London usually acts as the country's chief representative.

American Embassy *42 Elgin Road, Ballsbridge, Southern suburbs (668 8777/emergency number 668 9612/ www.dublin.usembassy.gov).* **Open** 8.30am-5pm Mon-Fri.

Australian Embassy *Fitzwilton House, Wilton Terrace (664 5300/www.ireland.embassy.gov.au).* **Open** 8.30am-4.30pm Mon-Fri.

British Embassy *29 Merrion Road, Ballsbridge, Southern suburbs (205 3700/emergency number 086 243 4655/www.britishembassy.ie).* **Open** 9.30am-5pm Mon-Fri.

Canadian Embassy *7-8 Wilton Terrace (294 4000/www.canada.ie).* **Open** 9am-4.30pm Mon-Fri.

New Zealand Consulate General *46 Upper Mount Street (all enquiries to New Zealand Embassy in London: 0044 207 9308 422/voice message service in Ireland 660 4233/www.mfat.govt.nz/ embassies).*

South African Embassy *Alexander House, Earlsfort Centre, Earlsfort Terrace (661 5553).* **Open** 8.30am-noon Mon-Fri.

Internet

Many hotels now offer some kind of internet access: luxury hotels should have broadband internet and wireless connection points in each room and hostels tend to have a clutch of terminals. Look out for the many cafés, bars and restaurants that provide wireless

as an added extra to customers. If you want to set up an internet account for your stay, good local ISPs include **Eircom Broadband** (1-800 242 633, www.eircom.ie) and **BT Broadband** (1-800 923 924, www.btireland.ie).

Internet access

If you can't get online in your hotel, you can guarantee that internet access won't be far away; Dublin is crawling with cybercafés, and most offer a decent number of terminals and other services such as printing, faxing and photocopying.

Central Café Internet *6 Grafton Street (677 8298/www.centralcafe.ie).* **Open** 9am-10pm Mon-Fri; 10am-9pm Sat, Sun.

Global Café Internet *8 Lower O'Connell Street (878 0295/www.global cafe.ie). Open 8am-11pm Mon-Fri; 9am-11pm Sat; 10am-11pm Sun.*

Opening hours

General business hours are 9am to 5.30pm Monday to Friday. Banks are open 10am to 4pm Monday to Wednesday and Friday, and from 10am to 5pm on Thursday. Shops in the city centre generally open between 9.30am and 6pm on Monday, Tuesday, Wednesday, Friday and Saturday, and from 2pm to 6pm on Sunday, with late-night opening until 8pm on Thursday and Friday.

Hours during which alcohol can be sold have been tightened once more after an experiment in slackness resulted in excessive drinking and late-night violence; pubs are now usually open from 11.30am to 11.30pm Monday to Thursday, and 11.30am to 12.30am Friday and Saturday (though many pubs in Dublin have permission to open until 1.30pm and later) and noon to 11pm on Sunday. Under new law, children are allowed in

ESSENTIALS

pubs, with adults, until 9pm. This is however at the discretion of the pub owner, and you may see signs stating earlier times.

Police

City centre Garda stations are located at Pearse Street (666 9000), Store Street (666 8000), Fitzgibbon Street (666 8400) and Metropolitan HQ, Harcourt Square (666 6666); all are open 24 hours daily. Non-emergency confidential calls to the Garda can also be made on 1-800 666 111.

Post

Post boxes are green and many have two slots: one for 'Dublin Only' and one for 'All Other Places'. It costs 55c to post a letter, postcard or unsealed card (weighing up to 50g) inside Ireland, 82c to the UK, Europe and all other international destinations. All airmail letters – including those to the UK – should have a blue priority airmail (*aerphost*) label affixed: you can get these free at all post offices. Post is generally delivered in fairly quick order within Ireland itself, and you should expect letters sent from Dublin to reach their destination within a day. International mail varies: it takes several days for letters or parcels to reach Europe and about a week to reach the US, or slightly more than that to reach Australia, South Africa or New Zealand.

Generally speaking post offices are open from 9am to 5pm Monday to Friday. Larger branches are also open from 9am to 1pm on Saturday. This rule is not inviolable, as offices have varying opening hours. Note that many smaller post offices still close for lunch from 12.45pm to 2pm. The General Post Office (O'Connell Street, 705 7000, www.anpost.ie) is open from 8am to 8pm, Monday to Saturday.

Smoking

In March 2004 a wide-ranging law banning all smoking in the workplace came into effect in Ireland. It is viewed as the most far-reaching anti-smoking legislation in the world and has proved to be a big success. It prohibits smoking in any bar, restaurant or public space in the whole country. The effect has been dramatic: all Dublin pubs, for example, became no-smoking areas overnight. Most pubs and bars have an outdoor, heated and seated area for smokers. However, some pubs don't; get used to seeing small groups of people standing at bar doors having a puff.

Telephones

The dialling code for Dublin is 01, although you don't need to use the prefix if you're calling within the Dublin region itself. Local phone numbers in Dublin all consist of seven digits, though you'll notice that elsewhere in Ireland phone numbers may be either shorter or longer. As in the US, numbers with the prefix 1-800 are free.

All Dublin numbers listed in this book have been listed without the city code of 01. If you need to dial any of these numbers within Dublin, simply use the numbers as they appear in the listings. If you are dialling from outside Dublin but within Ireland, add 01 to the front of the numbers listed. If you are dialling from outside Ireland, you need to dial the international dialling code + 353, then the Dublin city code 1 (omitting the initial 0), then the number as it appears in the guide.

To make an international call from within Ireland, dial 00, then dial the appropriate international code for the country you're calling, and then dial the number itself, omitting the first 0 from the area code where appropriate.

Charges

If you have access to a private telephone, the charges for your calls will be significantly lower than they would be from your hotel or your mobile. Reduced rates are available for calls made between 6pm and 8am from Monday to Friday, and all day Saturday, Sunday and Bank Holidays. If you need to make international calls, try to wait until these off-peak hours, as it is considerably cheaper.

If you can't use a private phone, the next easiest way to make long-distance calls is to buy a phone card, available from newsagents and post offices, which you can use on public pay phones. The majority of pay phones only accept these cards, not cash. The cards are especially useful outside Dublin, where payphones of all kinds are scarce, and it's best to be prepared.

Directories

The *Golden Pages* is Dublin's equivalent of the *Yellow Pages*. You can search at www.goldenpages.ie to find addresses in a given area. The 'Independent Directory', distributed annually, is a smaller version, with the added bonus of fairly good restaurant listings.

Mobile phones

There are several mobile networks in Ireland. Vodafone Ireland, O2, Meteor and Three each have about 98 per cent coverage across the country. Ireland's network uses the 900 and 1800 GSM bands, and

a UK handset will therefore work in Ireland as long as you have a roaming agreement with your service provider. Holders of US phones (usually 1900 GSM) should contact their service provider to check compatibility.

If you find you need to buy a mobile phone, or if you need to buy a new handset for your existing service, or if you want to sign up to an Irish mobile phone network, there are plenty of options. If you're here for just a short period of time, contact one of the following companies and get a pay-as-you-go phone that lets you buy talk time in advance. If you intend to rent a mobile phone to use during a short stay in the country, contact the Dublin Tourist Information office for a list of vendors.

Operator services

Dial **10** to reach the operator for Ireland and the UK, and **114** for international assistance.

Reverse-charge ('collect') calls are available via 1-800 55 88 90 and cost extra. For directory enquiries, dial 11811 or 11850 for Ireland and Northern Ireland, and 11818 for international numbers, including UK numbers. UK visitors planning their trip should note that when calling directory enquiries from the UK, Irish numbers are now listed on the myriad UK directory enquiries numbers, not under international directory enquiries.

Public phones

Cash- and card-operated pay phones are found in phone boxes across the city. They're not cheap, however, as a local telephone call from a pay phone generally costs 25c a minute; calls to mobiles are 50c a minute. A minimum €1 charge applies.

Tickets

Ticketmaster (0818 719 300/ from outside Ireland 456 9569/ www.ticketmaster.ie), in the St Stephen's Green shopping centre, deals with nearly every big event; the **Tourism Centre** can make credit card bookings (605 7729/ www.visitdublin.com); and tickets can often be bought at record shops.

Time

Ireland is in the same time zone as Britain, so it runs to Greenwich Mean Time. In spring, on a Saturday towards the end of March (exactly as happens in the UK and the US) the clocks go forward one hour for Summer Time. Clocks return to GMT towards the end of October, on the same day as the UK.

Tipping

You should tip between 12 and 15 per cent in restaurants. However, if – as is often the case – a service charge is included on your bill, ask waitstaff if they actually receive that money: you have every right to refuse to pay it if they don't. Always pay the tip in cash where you can, to make sure the people it's intended for get it.

Tip hairdressers and beauticians if you feel like it, and don't feel obliged to tip taxi drivers. A lot of city bars and clubs now have attendants in their lavatories, but don't feel that you have to tip them.

Tourist information

Set in a lovely converted church, the almost absurdly helpful **Dublin Tourist Centre** will do just about everything but your laundry. It has a bureau de change, car rental agency, booking service for tours and travel excursions, booking desk for concerts, theatre performances and other events, a friendly café, and a surprisingly good souvenir shop with fair prices.

You can also book hotel rooms here, though you'll have to pay a booking fee for each booking. To make a booking before you arrive, look online at www.goireland.com.

You might check out the **Dublin Pass** (www.dublinpass.ie), a smart card which, for a fee, gets you in 'free' to sights across the city. How affordable it is depends on how much you plan to see – prices start at €31 for a one-day card to €89 for a six-day pass.

Dublin Tourism Centre *St Andrew's Church, Suffolk Street, around Trinity College (1-850 230 330/0800 039 7000 from the UK/www.visitdublin. com). All cross-city buses.* **Open** *Jan-May, Oct-Dec* 9am-5.30pm Mon-Sat; 10.30am-3pm Sun. *June* 9am-7pm Mon-Sat; 10.30am-3pm Sun. *July* 9am-7pm Mon-Sat; 10.30am-5pm Sun.

Irish Tourist Board *Information 1-850 230 330 from within Ireland; UK office 0800 039 7000/www.Ireland.ie. Call centre: 24 hrs daily. Walk-in centre Nation House, 103 Wigmore Street, London.* **Open** 9am-5pm Mon-Fri.

Other tourism centres

You'll find tourist information centres at 14 Upper O'Connell Street; Baggot Street Bridge; Dublin Airport; and Dún Laoghaire Ferry Terminal.

What's on

Hot Press (www.hotpress.com) is fortnightly. It remains the best guide to the Dublin music scene, with comprehensive listings and reviews, and its debate pages are pretty lively. Alternatives to *Hot Press* include the amiable and very comprehensive *Event Guide*, a handy freesheet available in central cafés and bars.

Index

Sights

c

Campus Tours 49
Chester Beatty Library 55
Christ Church Cathedral 58
City Hall 58
Custom House Visitor
  Centre 110

d

Dalkey 123
Douglas Hyde Gallery 49
Dublin Castle 59
Dublinia 59
Dublin Writers' Museum
  90
Dublin Zoo 102
Dún Laoghaire 125

g

General Post Office 90
Guinness Storehouse 116

h

Howth 125
Hugh Lane Gallery
  (Municipal Gallery
  of Modern Art) 91

i

Irish Museum of Modern
  Art 116

j

James Joyce Centre 91
Jeanie Johnston 114
Jewish Museum 73

k

Kilkenny 128
Kilkenny Castle 129
Kilmainham Gaol 117
Knowth 129

l

Leinster House 77
Liberty Hall 111

m

Malahide 125

n

National Gallery
  of Ireland 77
National Library
  of Ireland 77
National Museum
  of Archaeology
  & History 77
National Museum of
  Ireland: Decorative
  Arts & History 103
National Print Museum 77
Newgrange 129
Newman House 78
Newman University
  Church 78
Number Twenty-Nine 78

o

Old Jameson Distillery
  104
Old Library & Book
  of Kells 50
Oscar Wilde House 78

p

Phoenix Park Visitors'
  Centre 104

r

Rothe House 129

s

Sandycove 125
Sandymount 125
Science Gallery 51
Seapoint 125
St Canice's Cathedral 129
St Michan's Church 104
St Patrick's Cathedral 59

t

Trinity College 48

w

War Memorial Gardens
  119
Whitefriar Street
  Carmelite Church 59
Wicklow Gaol 132
Wicklow Mountains 132

Eating & drinking

101 Talbot 91

b

Bald Barista 59
Ba Mizu 59
Bang Café 78
Bar Italia
Bernard Shaw Bar 78
Bewley's Oriental Café
  61
Bleeding Horse 79
Bóbó's 79
Brick Alley Café 61
Bruxelles 61

c

Café Cagliostro 92
Cake Café 79
Canal Bank Café 80
Carluccio's 61
Cellar 80
Chancery 105
Chapter One 92
Cobalt Café 93
Cobblestone 105
Corner Stone 80
Cornucopia 62

d

Dakota 62
Da Vincenzo 80
Davy Byrnes 62
DAX 81
Diep Le Shaker 81
Dobbins 81
Doheny & Nesbitt 81
Dunne & Crescenzi 62

e

Ecrivain, L' 81
Ely 81
Enoteca delle Langhe
  93

f

Farm 63
Fitzers 63
Flannery's 81
Floridita 93
Flowing Tide 94

ESSENTIALS

ESSENTIALS